DAN-70   DANTES SUBJECT STANDARDIZED TESTS (DSST)

This is your
PASSBOOK for...

The Civil War and Reconstruction

Test Preparation Study Guide
Questions & Answers

COPYRIGHT NOTICE

This book is SOLELY intended for, is sold ONLY to, and its use is RESTRICTED to individual, bona fide applicants or candidates who qualify by virtue of having seriously filed applications for appropriate license, certificate, professional and/or promotional advancement, higher school matriculation, scholarship, or other legitimate requirements of education and/or governmental authorities.

This book is NOT intended for use, class instruction, tutoring, training, duplication, copying, reprinting, excerption, or adaptation, etc., by:

1) Other publishers
2) Proprietors and/or Instructors of "Coaching" and/or Preparatory Courses
3) Personnel and/or Training Divisions of commercial, industrial, and governmental organizations
4) Schools, colleges, or universities and/or their departments and staffs, including teachers and other personnel
5) Testing Agencies or Bureaus
6) Study groups which seek by the purchase of a single volume to copy and/or duplicate and/or adapt this material for use by the group as a whole without having purchased individual volumes for each of the members of the group
7) Et al.

Such persons would be in violation of appropriate Federal and State statutes.

PROVISION OF LICENSING AGREEMENTS – Recognized educational, commercial, industrial, and governmental institutions and organizations, and others legitimately engaged in educational pursuits, including training, testing, and measurement activities, may address request for a licensing agreement to the copyright owners, who will determine whether, and under what conditions, including fees and charges, the materials in this book may be used them. In other words, a licensing facility exists for the legitimate use of the material in this book on other than an individual basis. However, it is asseverated and affirmed here that the material in this book CANNOT be used without the receipt of the express permission of such a licensing agreement from the Publishers. Inquiries re licensing should be addressed to the company, attention rights and permissions department.

All rights reserved, including the right of reproduction in whole or in part, in any form or by any means, electronic or mechanical, including photocopying, recording, or by any information storage and retrieval system, without permission in writing from the Publisher.

Copyright © 2024 by
National Learning Corporation

212 Michael Drive, Syosset, NY 11791
(516) 921-8888 • www.passbooks.com
E-mail: info@passbooks.com

PUBLISHED IN THE UNITED STATES OF AMERICA

PASSBOOK® SERIES

THE *PASSBOOK® SERIES* has been created to prepare applicants and candidates for the ultimate academic battlefield – the examination room.

At some time in our lives, each and every one of us may be required to take an examination – for validation, matriculation, admission, qualification, registration, certification, or licensure.

Based on the assumption that every applicant or candidate has met the basic formal educational standards, has taken the required number of courses, and read the necessary texts, the *PASSBOOK® SERIES* furnishes the one special preparation which may assure passing with confidence, instead of failing with insecurity. Examination questions – together with answers – are furnished as the basic vehicle for study so that the mysteries of the examination and its compounding difficulties may be eliminated or diminished by a sure method.

This book is meant to help you pass your examination provided that you qualify and are serious in your objective.

The entire field is reviewed through the huge store of content information which is succinctly presented through a provocative and challenging approach – the question-and-answer method.

A climate of success is established by furnishing the correct answers at the end of each test.

You soon learn to recognize types of questions, forms of questions, and patterns of questioning. You may even begin to anticipate expected outcomes.

You perceive that many questions are repeated or adapted so that you can gain acute insights, which may enable you to score many sure points.

You learn how to confront new questions, or types of questions, and to attack them confidently and work out the correct answers.

You note objectives and emphases, and recognize pitfalls and dangers, so that you may make positive educational adjustments.

Moreover, you are kept fully informed in relation to new concepts, methods, practices, and directions in the field.

You discover that you are actually taking the examination all the time: you are preparing for the examination by "taking" an examination, not by reading extraneous and/or supererogatory textbooks.

In short, this PASSBOOK®, used directedly, should be an important factor in helping you to pass your test.

NONTRADITIONAL EDUCATION

Students returning to school as adults bring more varied experience to their studies than do the teenagers who begin college shortly after graduating from high school. As a result, there are numerous programs for students with nontraditional learning curves. Hundreds of colleges and universities grant degrees to people who cannot attend classes at a regular campus or have already learned what the college is supposed to teach.

You can earn nontraditional education credits in many ways:
- Passing standardized exams
- Demonstrating knowledge gained through experience
- Completing campus-based coursework, and
- Taking courses off campus

Some methods of assessing learning for credit are objective, such as standardized tests. Others are more subjective, such as a review of life experiences.

With some help from four hypothetical characters – Alice, Vin, Lynette, and Jorge – this article describes nontraditional ways of earning educational credit. It begins by describing programs in which you can earn a high school diploma without spending 4 years in a classroom. The college picture is more complicated, so it is presented in two parts: one on gaining credit for what you know through course work or experience, and a second on college degree programs. The final section lists resources for locating more information.

Earning High School Credit

People who were prevented from finishing high school as teenagers have several options if they want to do so as adults. Some major cities have back-to-school programs that allow adults to attend high school classes with current students. But the more practical alternatives for most adults are to take the General Educational Development (GED) tests or to earn a high school diploma by demonstrating their skills or taking correspondence classes.

Of course, these options do not match the experience of staying in high school and graduating with one's friends. But they are viable alternatives for adult learners committed to meeting and, often, continuing their educational goals.

GED Program

Alice quit high school her sophomore year and took a job to help support herself, her younger brother, and their newly widowed mother. Now an adult, she wants to earn her high school diploma – and then go on to college. Because her job as head cook and her family responsibilities keep her busy during the day, she plans to get a high school equivalency diploma. She will study for, and take, the GED tests. Every year, about half a million adults earn their high school credentials this way. A GED diploma is accepted in lieu of a high school one by more than 90 percent of employers, colleges, and universities, so it is a good choice for someone like Alice.

The GED testing program is sponsored by the American Council on Education and State and local education departments. It consists of examinations in five subject areas: Writing, science, mathematics, social studies, and literature and the arts. The tests also measure skills such as analytical ability, problem solving, reading comprehension, and ability to understand and apply information. Most of the questions are multiple choice; the writing test includes an essay section on a topic of general interest.

Eligibility rules for taking the exams vary, but some states require that you must be at least 18. Tests are given in English, Spanish, and French. In addition to standard print, versions in large print, Braille, and audiocassette are also available. Total time allotted for the tests is 7 1/2 hours.

The GED tests are not easy. About one-fourth of those who complete the exams every year do not pass. Passing scores are established by administering the tests to a sample of graduating high school seniors. The minimum standard score is set so that about one-third of graduating seniors would not pass the tests if they took them.

Because of the difficulty of the tests, people need to prepare themselves to take them. Often, they start by taking the Official GED Practice Tests, usually available through a local adult education center. Centers are listed in your phone book's blue pages under "Adult Education," "Continuing Education," or "GED." Adult education centers also have information about GED preparation classes and self-study materials. Classes are generally arranged to accommodate adults' work schedules. National Learning Corporation publishes several study guides that aim to thoroughly prepare test-takers for the GED.

School districts, colleges, adult education centers, and community organizations have information about GED testing schedules and practice tests. For more information, contact them, your nearest GED testing center, or:

GED Testing Service
One Dupont Circle, NW, Suite 250
Washington, DC 20036-1163
1(800) 62-MY GED (626-9433)
(202) 939-9490

Skills Demonstration

Adults who have acquired high school level skills through experience might be eligible for the National External Diploma Program. This alternative to the GED does not involve any direct instruction. Instead, adults seeking a high school diploma must demonstrate mastery of 65 competencies in 8 general areas: Communication; computation; occupational preparedness; and self, social, consumer, scientific, and technological awareness.

Mastery is shown through the completion of the tasks. For example, a participant could prove competency in computation by measuring a room for carpeting, figuring out the amount of carpet needed, and computing the cost.

Before being accepted for the program, adults undergo an evaluation. Tests taken at one of the program's offices measure reading, writing, and mathematics abilities. A take-home segment includes a self-assessment of current skills, an individual skill evaluation, and an occupational interest and aptitude test.

Adults accepted for the program have weekly meetings with an assessor. At the meeting, the assessor reviews the participant's work from the previous week. If the task has not been completed properly, the assessor explains the mistake. Participants continue to correct their errors until they master each competency. A high school diploma is awarded upon proven mastery of all 65 competencies.

Fourteen States and the District of Columbia now offer the External Diploma Program. For more information, contact:

External Diploma Program
One Dupont Circle, NW, Suite 250
Washington, DC 20036-1193
(202) 939-9475

Correspondence and Distance Study

Vin dropped out of high school during his junior year because his family's frequent moves made it difficult for him to continue his studies. He promised himself at the time he dropped out that he would someday finish the courses needed for his diploma. For people like Vin, who prefer to earn a traditional diploma in a nontraditional way, there are about a dozen accredited courses of study for earning a high school diploma by correspondence, or distance study. The programs are either privately run, affiliated with a university, or administered by a State education department.

Distance study diploma programs have no residency requirements, allowing students to continue their studies from almost any location. Depending on the course of study, students need not be enrolled full time and usually have more flexible schedules for finishing their work. Selection of courses ranges from vo-tech to college prep, and some programs place different emphasis on the types of diplomas offered. University affiliated schools, for example, allow qualified students to take college courses along with their high school ones. Students can then apply the college credits toward a degree at that university or transfer them to another institution.

Taking courses by distance study is often more challenging and time consuming than attending classes, especially for adults who have other obligations. Success depends on each student's motivation. Students usually do reading assignments on their own. Written exercises, which they complete and send to an instructor for grading, supplement their reading material.

A list of some accredited high schools that offer diplomas by distance study is available free from the Distance Education and Training Council, formerly known as the National Home Study Council. Request the "DETC Directory of Accredited Institutions" from:

The Distance Education and Training Council
1601 18th Street, NW.
Washington, DC 20009-2529
(202) 234-5100

Some publications profiling nontraditional college programs include addresses and descriptions of several high school correspondence ones. See the Resources section at the end of this article for more information.

Getting College Credit For What You Know

Adults can receive college credit for prior coursework, by passing examinations, and documenting experiential learning. With help from a college advisor, nontraditional students should assess their skills, establish their educational goals, and determine the number of college credits they might be eligible for.

Even before you meet with a college advisor, you should collect all your school and training records. Then, make a list of all knowledge and abilities acquired through experience, no matter how irrelevant they seem to your chosen field. Next, determine your educational goals: What specific field do you wish to study? What kind of a degree do you want? Finally, determine how your past work fits into the field of study. Later on, you will evaluate educational programs to find one that's right for you.

People who have complex educational or experiential learning histories might want to have their learning evaluated by the Regents Credit Bank. The Credit Bank, operated by Regents College of the University of the State of New York, allows people to consolidate credits earned through college, experience, or other methods. Special assessments are available for Regents College enrollees whose knowledge in a specific field cannot be adequately evaluated by standardized exams. For more information, contact the Regents Credit Bank at:

Regents College
7 Columbia Circle
Albany, NY 12203-5159
(518) 464-8500

Credit For Prior College Coursework

When Lynette was in college during the 1970s, she attended several different schools and took a variety of courses. She did well in some classes and poorly in others. Now that she is a successful business owner and has more focus, Lynette thinks she should forget about her previous coursework and start from scratch. Instead, she should start from where she is.

Lynette should have all her transcripts sent to the colleges or universities of her choice and let an admissions officer determine which classes are applicable toward a degree. A few credits here and there may not seem like much, but they add up. Even if the subjects do not seem relevant to any major, they might be counted as elective credits toward a degree. And comparing the cost of transcripts with the cost of college courses, it makes sense to spend a few dollars per transcript for a chance to save hundreds, and perhaps thousands, of dollars in books and tuition.

Rules for transferring credits apply to all prior coursework at accredited colleges and universities, whether done on campus or off. Courses completed off campus, often called extended learning, include those available to students through independent study and correspondence. Many schools have extended learning programs; Brigham Young University, for example, offers more than 300 courses through its Department of Independent Study. One type of extended learning is distance learning, a form of correspondence study by technological means such as television, video and audio, CD-ROM, electronic mail, and computer tutorials. See the Resources section at the end of this article for more information about publications available from the National University Continuing Education Association.

Any previously earned college credits should be considered for transfer, no matter what the subject or the grade received. Many schools do not accept the transfer of courses graded below a C or ones taken more than a designated number of years ago. Some colleges and universities also have limits on the number of credits that can be transferred and applied toward a degree. But not all do. For example, Thomas Edison State College, New Jersey's State college for adults, accepts the transfer of all 120 hours of credit required for a baccalaureate degree – provided all the credits are transferred from regionally accredited schools, no more than 80 are at the junior college level, and the student's grades overall and in the field of study average out to C.

To assign credit for prior coursework, most schools require original transcripts. This means you must complete a form or send a written, signed request to have your transcripts released directly to a college or university. Once you have chosen the schools you want to apply to, contact the schools you attended before. Find out how much each transcript costs, and ask them to send your transcripts to the ones you are applying to. Write a letter that includes your name (and names used during attendance, if different) and dates of attendance, along with the names and addresses of the schools to which your transcripts should be sent. Include payment and mail to the registrar at the schools you have attended. The registrar's office will process your request and send an official transcript of your coursework to the colleges or universities you have designated.

Credit For Noncollege Courses

Colleges and universities are not the only ones that offer classes. Volunteer organizations and employers often provide formal training worth college credit. The American Council on Education has two programs that assess thousands of specific courses and make recommendations on the amount of college credit they are worth. Colleges and universities accept the recommendations or use them as guidelines.

One program evaluates educational courses sponsored by government agencies, business and industry, labor unions, and professional and voluntary organizations. It is the Program on Noncollegiate Sponsored Instruction (PONSI). Some of the training seminars Alice has participated in covered topics such as food preparation, kitchen safety, and nutrition. Although she has not yet earned her GED, Alice can earn college credit because of her completion of these formal job-training seminars. The number of credits each seminar is worth does not hinge on Alice's current eligibility for college enrollment.

The other program evaluates courses offered by the Army, Navy, Air Force, Marines, Coast Guard, and Department of Defense. It is the Military Evaluations Program. Jorge has never attended college, but the engineering technology classes he completed as part of his military training are worth college credit. And as an Army veteran, Jorge is eligible for a service that takes the evaluations one step further. The Army/American Council on Education Registry Transcript System (AARTS) will provide Jorge with an individualized transcript of American Council on Education credit recommendations for all courses he completed, the military occupational specialties (MOS's) he held, and examinations he passed while in the Army. All Army and National Guard enlisted personnel and veterans who enlisted after October 1981 are eligible for the transcript. Similar services are being considered by the Navy and Marine Corps.

To obtain a free transcript, see your Army Education Center for a 5454R transcript request form. Include your name, Social Security number, basic active service date, and complete address where you want the transcript sent. Mail your request to:

AARTS Operations Center
415 McPherson Ave.
Fort Leavenworth, KS 66027-1373

Recommendations for PONSI are published in *The National Guide to Educational Credit for Training Programs;* military program recommendations are in *The Guide to the Evaluation of Educational Experiences in the Armed Forces.* See the Resources section at the end of this article for more information about these publications.

Former military personnel who took a foreign language course through the Defense Language Institute may request course transcripts by sending their name, Social Security number, course title, duration of the course, and graduation date to:

Commandant, Defense Language Institute
Attn: ATFL-DAA-AR
Transcripts
Presidio of Monterey
Monterey, CA 93944-5006

Not all of Jorge's and Alice's courses have been assessed by the American Council on Education. Training courses that have no Council credit recommendation should still be assessed by an advisor at the schools they want to attend. Course descriptions, class notes, test scores, and other documentation may be helpful for comparing training courses to their college equivalents. An oral examination or other demonstration of competency might also be required.

There is no guarantee you will receive all the credits you are seeking – but you certainly won't if you make no attempt.

Credit By Examination

Standardized tests are the best-known method of receiving college credit without taking courses. These exams are often taken by high school students seeking advanced placement for college, but they are also available to adult learners. Testing programs and colleges and universities offer exams in a number of subjects. Two U.S. Government institutes have foreign language exams for employees that also may be worth college credit.

It is important to understand that receiving a passing score on these exams does not mean you get college credit automatically. Each school determines which test results it will accept, minimum scores required, how scores are converted for credit, and the amount of credit, if any, to be assigned. Most colleges and universities accept the American Council on Education credit recommendations, published every other year in the 250-page *Guide to Educational Credit by Examination*. For more information, contact:

The American Council on Education
Credit by Examination Program
One Dupont Circle, Suite 250
Washington, DC 20036-1193
(202) 939-9434

Testing programs:

You might know some of the five national testing programs by their acronyms or initials: CLEP, ACT PEP: RCE, DANTES, AP, and NOCTI. (The meanings of these initialisms are explained below.) There is some overlap among programs; for example, four of them have introductory accounting exams. Since you will not be awarded credit more than once for a specific subject, you should carefully evaluate each program for the subject exams you wish to take. And before taking an exam, make sure you will be awarded credit by the college or university you plan to attend.

CLEP (College-Level Examination Program), administered by the College Board, is the most widely accepted of the national testing programs; more than 2,800 accredited schools award credit for passing exam scores. Each test covers material taught in basic undergraduate courses. There are five general exams – English composition, humanities, college mathematics, natural sciences, and social sciences and history – and many subject exams. Most exams are entirely multiple-choice, but English composition exams may include an essay section. For more information, contact:

    CLEP
    P.O. Box 6600
    Princeton, NJ 08541-6600
    (609) 771-7865

ACT PEP: RCE (American College Testing Proficiency Exam Program: Regents College Examinations) tests are given in 38 subjects within arts and sciences, business, education, and nursing. Each exam is recommended for either lower- or upper-level credit. Exams contain either objective or extended response questions, and are graded according to a standard score, letter grade, or pass/fail. Fees vary, depending on the subject and type of exam. For more information or to request free study guides, contact:

    ACT PEP: Regents College Examinations
    P.O. Box 4014
    Iowa City, IA 52243
    (319) 337-1387
    (New York State residents must contact Regents College directly.)

DANTES (Defense Activity for Nontraditional Education Support) standardized tests are developed by the Educational Testing Service for the Department of Defense. Originally administered only to military personnel, the exams have been available to the public since 1983. About 50 subject tests cover business, mathematics, social science, physical science, humanities, foreign languages, and applied technology. Most of the tests consist entirely of multiple-choice questions. Schools determine their own administering fees and testing schedules. For more information or to request free study sheets, contact:

    DANTES Program Office
    Mail Stop 31-X
    Educational Testing Service
    Princeton, NJ 08541
    1(800) 257-9484

The AP (Advanced Placement) Program is a cooperative effort between secondary schools and colleges and universities. AP exams are developed each year by committees of college and high school faculty appointed by the College Board and assisted by consultants from the Educational Testing Service. Subjects include arts and languages, natural sciences, computer science, social sciences, history, and mathematics. Most tests are 2 or 3 hours long and include both multiple-choice and essay questions. AP courses are available to help students prepare for exams, which are offered in the spring. For more information about the Advanced Placement Program, contact:

    Advanced Placement Services
    P.O. Box 6671
    Princeton, NJ 08541-6671
    (609) 771-7300

NOCTI (National Occupational Competency Testing Institute) assessments are designed for people like Alice, who have vocational-technical skills that cannot be evaluated by other tests. NOCTI assesses competency at two levels: Student/job ready and teacher/experienced worker. Standardized evaluations are available for occupations such as auto-body repair, electronics, mechanical drafting, quantity food preparation, and upholstering. The tests consist of multiple-choice questions and a performance component. Other services include workshops, customized assessments, and pre-testing. For more information, contact:

NOCTI
500 N. Bronson Ave.
Ferris State University
Big Rapids, MI 49307
(616) 796-4699

Colleges and universities:

Many colleges and universities have credit-by-exam programs, through which students earn credit by passing a comprehensive exam for a course offered by the institution. Among the most widely recognized are the programs at Ohio University, the University of North Carolina, Thomas Edison State College, and New York University.

Ohio University offers about 150 examinations for credit. In addition, you may sometimes arrange to take special examinations in non-laboratory courses offered at Ohio University. To take a test for credit, you must enroll in the course. If you plan to transfer the credit earned, you also need written permission from an official at your school. Books and study materials are available, for a cost, through the university. Exams must be taken within 6 months of the enrollment date; most last 3 hours. You may arrange to take the exam off campus if you do not live near the university.

Ohio University is on the quarter-hour system; most courses are worth 4 quarter hours, the equivalent of 3 semester hours. For more information, contact:

Independent Study
Tupper Hall 302
Ohio University
Athens, OH 45701-2979
1(800) 444-2910
(614) 593-2910

The University of North Carolina offers a credit-by-examination option for 140 independent study (correspondence) courses in foreign languages, humanities, social sciences, mathematics, business administration, education, electrical and computer engineering, health administration, and natural sciences. To take an exam, you must request and receive approval from both the course instructor and the independent studies department. Exams must be taken within six months of enrollment, and you may register for no more than two at a time. If you are not near the University's Chapel Hill campus, you may take your exam under supervision at an accredited college, university, community college, or technical institute. For more information, contact:

Independent Studies
CB #1020, The Friday Center
UNC-Chapel Hill
Chapel Hill, NC 27599-1020
1(800) 862-5669 / (919) 962-1134

The Thomas Edison College Examination Program offers more than 50 exams in liberal arts, business, and professional areas. Thomas Edison State College administers tests twice a month in Trenton, New Jersey; however, students may arrange to take their tests with a proctor at any accredited American college or university or U.S. military base. Most of the tests are multiple choice; some also include short answer or essay questions. Time limits range from 90 minutes to 4 hours, depending on the exam. For more information, contact:

Thomas Edison State College
TECEP, Office of Testing and Assessment
101 W. State Street
Trenton, NJ 08608-1176
(609) 633-2844

New York University's Foreign Language Program offers proficiency exams in more than 40 languages, from Albanian to Yiddish. Two exams are available in each language: The 12-point test is equivalent to 4 undergraduate semesters, and the 16-point exam may lead to upper level credit. The tests are given at the university's Foreign Language Department throughout the year.

Proof of foreign language proficiency does not guarantee college credit. Some colleges and universities accept transcripts only for languages commonly taught, such as French and Spanish. Nontraditional programs are more likely than traditional ones to grant credit for proficiency in other languages.

For an informational brochure and registration form for NYU's foreign language proficiency exams, contact:

New York University
Foreign Language Department
48 Cooper Square, Room 107
New York, NY 10003
(212) 998-7030

Government institutes:

The Defense Language Institute and Foreign Service Institute administer foreign language proficiency exams for personnel stationed abroad. Usually, the tests are given at the end of intensive language courses or upon completion of service overseas. But some people – like Jorge, who knows Spanish – speak another language fluently and may be allowed to take a proficiency exam in that language before completing their tour of duty. Contact one of the offices listed below to obtain transcripts of those scores. Proof of proficiency does not guarantee college credit, however, as discussed above.

To request score reports from the Defense Language Institute for Defense Language Proficiency Tests, send your name, Social Security number, language for which you were tested, and, most importantly, when and where you took the exam to:

Commandant, Defense Language Institute
Attn: ATFL-ES-T
DLPT Score Report Request
Presidio of Monterey
Monterey, CA 93944-5006

To request transcripts of scores for Foreign Service Institute exams, send your name, Social Security number, language for which you were tested, and dates or year of exams to:

Foreign Service Institute
Arlington Hall
4020 Arlington Boulevard
Rosslyn, VA 22204-1500
Attn: Testing Office (Send your request to the attention of the testing office of the foreign language in which you were tested)

Credit For Experience

Experiential learning credit may be given for knowledge gained through job responsibilities, personal hobbies, volunteer opportunities, homemaking, and other experiences. Colleges and universities base credit awards on the knowledge you have attained, not for the experience alone. In addition, the knowledge must be college level; not just any learning will do. Throwing horseshoes as a hobby is not likely to be worth college credit. But if you've done research on how and where the sport originated, visited blacksmiths, organized tournaments, and written a column for a trade journal – well, that's a horseshoe of a different color.

Adults attempting to get credit for their experience should be forewarned: Having your experience evaluated for college credit is time-consuming, tedious work – not an easy shortcut for people who want quick-fix college credits. And not all experience, no matter how valuable, is the equivalent of college courses.

Requesting college credit for your experiential learning can be tricky. You should get assistance from a credit evaluations officer at the school you plan to attend, but you should also have a general idea of what your knowledge is worth. A common method for converting knowledge into credit is to use a college catalog. Find course titles and descriptions that match what you have learned through experience, and request the number of credits offered for those courses.

Once you know what credit to ask for, you must usually present your case in writing to officials at the college you plan to attend. The most common form of presenting experiential learning for credit is the portfolio. A portfolio is a written record of your knowledge along with a request for equivalent college credit. It includes an identification and description of the knowledge for which you are requesting credit, an explanatory essay of how the knowledge was gained and how it fits into your educational plans, documentation that you have acquired such knowledge, and a request for college credit. Required elements of a portfolio vary by schools but generally follow those guidelines.

In identifying knowledge you have gained, be specific about exactly what you have learned. For example, it is not enough for Lynette to say she runs a business. She must identify the knowledge she has gained from running it, such as personnel management, tax law, marketing strategy, and inventory review. She must also include brief descriptions about her knowledge of each to support her claims of having those skills.

The essay gives you a chance to relay something about who you are. It should address your educational goals, include relevant autobiographical details, and be well organized, neat, and convey confidence. In his essay, Jorge might first state his goal of becoming an engineer. Then he would explain why he joined the Army, where he got hands-on training and experience in developing and servicing electronic equipment.

This, he would say, led to his hobby of creating remote-controlled model cars, of which he has built 20. His conclusion would highlight his accomplishments and tie them to his desire to become an electronic engineer.

Documentation is evidence that you've learned what you claim to have learned. You can show proof of knowledge in a variety of ways, including audio or video recordings, letters from current or former employers describing your specific duties and job performance, blueprints, photographs or artwork, and transcripts of certifying exams for professional licenses and certification – such as Alice's certification from the American Culinary Federation. Although documentation can take many forms, written proof alone is not always enough. If it is impossible to document your knowledge in writing, find out if your experiential learning can be assessed through supplemental oral exams by a faculty expert.

Earning a College Degree

Nontraditional students often have work, family, and financial obligations that prevent them from quitting their jobs to attend school full time. Can they still meet their educational goals? Yes.

More than 150 accredited colleges and universities have nontraditional bachelor's degree programs that require students to spend little or no time on campus; over 300 others have nontraditional campus-based degree programs. Some of those schools, as well as most junior and community colleges, offer associate's degrees nontraditionally. Each school with a nontraditional course of study determines its own rules for awarding credit for prior coursework, exams, or experience, as discussed previously. Most have charges on top of tuition for providing these special services.

Several publications profile nontraditional degree programs; see the Resources section at the end of this article for more information. To determine which school best fits your academic profile and educational goals, first list your criteria. Then, evaluate nontraditional programs based on their accreditation, features, residency requirements, and expenses. Once you have chosen several schools to explore further, write to them for more information. Detailed explanations of school policies should help you decide which ones you want to apply to.

Get beyond the printed word – especially the glowing words each school writes about itself. Check out the schools you are considering with higher education authorities, alumni, employers, family members, and friends. If possible, visit the campus to talk to students and instructors and sit in on a few classes, even if you will be completing most or all of your work off campus. Ask school officials questions about such things as enrollment numbers, graduation rate, faculty qualifications, and confusing details about the application process or academic policies. After you have thoroughly investigated each prospective college or university, you can make an informed decision about which is right for you.

Accreditation

Accreditation is a process colleges and universities submit to voluntarily for getting their credentials. An accredited school has been investigated and visited by teams of observers and has periodic inspections by a private accrediting agency. The initial review can take two years or more.

Regional agencies accredit entire schools, and professional agencies accredit either specialized schools or departments within schools. Although there are no national accrediting standards, not just any accreditation will do. Countless "accreditation associations" have been invented by schools, many of which have no academic programs and sell phony degrees, to accredit themselves. But 6 regional and about 80 professional accrediting associations in the United States are recognized by the U.S. Department of Education or the Commission on Recognition of Postsecondary Accreditation. When checking accreditation, these are the names to look for. For more information about accreditation and accrediting agencies, contact:

> Institutional Participation Oversight Service Accreditation and State Liaison Division
> U.S. Department of Education
> ROB 3, Room 3915
> 600 Independence Ave., SW
> Washington, DC 20202-5244
> (202) 708-7417

Because accreditation is not mandatory, lack of accreditation does not necessarily mean a school or program is bad. Some schools choose not to apply for accreditation, are in the process of applying, or have educational methods too unconventional for an accrediting association's standards. For the nontraditional student, however, earning a degree from a college or university with recognized accreditation is an especially important consideration. Although nontraditional education is becoming more widely accepted, it is not yet mainstream. Employers skeptical of a degree earned in a nontraditional manner are likely to be even less accepting of one from an unaccredited school.

Program Features

Because nontraditional students have diverse educational objectives, nontraditional schools are diverse in what they offer. Some programs are geared toward helping students organize their scattered educational credits to get a degree as quickly as possible. Others cater to those who may have specific credits or experience but need assistance in completing requirements. Whatever your educational profile, you should look for a program that works with you in obtaining your educational goals.

A few nontraditional programs have special admissions policies for adult learners like Alice, who plan to earn their GEDs but want to enroll in college in the meantime. Other features of nontraditional programs include individualized learning agreements, intensive academic counseling, cooperative learning and internship placement, and waiver of some prerequisites or other requirements – as well as college credit for prior coursework, examinations, and experiential learning, all discussed previously.

Lynette, whose primary goal is to finish her degree, wants to earn maximum credits for her business experience. She will look for programs that do not limit the number of credits awarded for equivalency exams and experiential learning. And since well-documented proof of knowledge is essential for earning experiential learning credits, Lynette should make sure the program she chooses provides assistance to students submitting a portfolio.

Jorge, on the other hand, has more credits than he needs in certain areas and is willing to forego some. To become an engineer, he must have a bachelor's degree; but because he is accustomed to hands-on learning, Jorge is interested in getting experience as he gains more technical skills. He will concentrate on finding schools with strong cooperative education, supervised fieldwork, or internship programs.

Residency Requirements

Programs are sometimes deemed nontraditional because of their residency requirements. Many people think of residency for colleges and universities in terms of tuition, with in-state students paying less than out-of-state ones. Residency also may refer to where a student lives, either on or off campus, while attending school.

But in nontraditional education, residency usually refers to how much time students must spend on campus, regardless of whether they attend classes there. In some nontraditional programs, students need not ever step foot on campus. Others require only a very short residency, such as one day or a few weeks. Many schools have standard residency requirements of several semesters but schedule classes for evenings or weekends to accommodate working adults.

Lynette, who previously took courses by independent study, prefers to earn credits by distance study. She will focus on schools that have no residency requirement. Several colleges and universities have nonresident degree completion programs for adults with some college credit. Under the direction of a faculty advisor, students devise a plan for earning their remaining credits. Methods for earning credits include independent study, distance learning, seminars, supervised fieldwork, and group study at arranged sites. Students may have to earn a certain number of credits through the degree-granting institution. But many programs allow students to take courses at accredited schools of their choice for transfer toward their degree.

Alice wants to attend lectures but has an unpredictable schedule. Her best course of action will be to seek out short residency programs that require students to attend seminars once or twice a semester. She can take courses that are televised and videotape them to watch when her schedule permits, with the seminars helping to ensure that she properly completes her coursework. Many colleges and universities with short residency requirements also permit students to earn some credits elsewhere, by whatever means the student chooses.

Some fields of study require classroom instruction. As Jorge will discover, few colleges and universities allow students to earn a bachelor's degree in engineering entirely through independent study. Nontraditional residency programs are designed to accommodate adults' daytime work schedules. Jorge should look for programs offering evening, weekend, summer, and accelerated courses.

Tuition and Other Expenses

The final decisions about which schools Alice, Jorge, and Lynette attend may hinge in large part on a single issue: Cost. And rising tuition is only part of the equation. Beginning with application fees and continuing through graduation fees, college expenses add up.

Traditional and nontraditional students have some expenses in common, such as the cost of books and other materials. Tuition might even be the same for some courses, especially for colleges and universities offering standard ones at unusual times. But for nontraditional programs, students may also pay fees for services such as credit or transcript review, evaluation, advisement, and portfolio assessment.

Students are also responsible for postage and handling or setup expenses for independent study courses, as well as for all examination and transcript fees for transferring credits. Usually, the more nontraditional the program, the more detailed the fees. Some schools charge a yearly enrollment fee rather than tuition for degree completion candidates who want their files to remain active.

Although tuition and fees might seem expensive, most educators tell you not to let money come between you and your educational goals. Talk to someone in the financial aid department of the school you plan to attend or check your library for publications about financial aid sources. The U.S. Department of Education publishes a guide to Federal aid programs such as Pell Grants, student loans, and work-study. To order the free 74-page booklet, *The Student Guide: Financial Aid from the U.S. Department of Education,* contact:

Federal Student Aid Information Center
P.O. Box 84
Washington, DC 20044
1 (800) 4FED-AID (433-3243)

Resources

Information on how to earn a high school diploma or college degree without following the usual routes is available from several organizations and in numerous publications. Information on nontraditional graduate degree programs, available for master's through doctoral level, though not discussed in this article, can usually be obtained from the same resources that detail bachelor's degree programs.

National Learning Corporation publishes study guides for all of these exams, for both general examinations and tests in specific subject areas. To order study guides, or to browse their catalog featuring more than 5,000 titles, visit NLC online at www.passbooks.com, or contact them by phone at (800) 632-8888.

Organizations

Adult learners should always contact their local school system, community college, or university to learn about programs that are readily available. The following national organizations can also supply information:

American Council on Education
One Dupont Circle
Washington, DC 20036-1193
(202) 939-9300

Within the American Council on Education, the Center for Adult Learning and Educational Credentials administers the National External Diploma Program, the GED Program, the Program on Noncollegiate Sponsored Instruction, the Credit by Examination Program, and the Military Evaluations Program.

DANTES Subject Standardized Tests

INTRODUCTION

The DANTES (Defense Activity for Non-Traditional Education Support) subject standardized tests are comprehensive college and graduate level examinations given by the Armed Forces, colleges and graduate schools as end-of-subject course evaluation final examinations or to obtain college equivalency credits in the various subject areas tested.

The DANTES Examination Program enables students to obtain college credit for what they have learned on the job, through self-study, personal interest, correspondence courses or by any other means. It is used by colleges and universities to award college credit to students who demonstrate that they know as much as students completing an equivalent college course. It is a cost-efficient, time-saving way for students to use their knowledge to accomplish their educational goals.

Most schools accept the American Council on Education (ACE) recommendations for the minimum score required and the amount of credit awarded, but not all schools do. Be sure to check the policy regarding the score level required for credit and the number of credits to be awarded.

Not all tests are accepted by all institutions. Even when a test is accepted by an institution, it may not be acceptable for every program at that institution. Before considering testing, ascertain the acceptability of a specific test for a particular course.

Colleges and universities that administer DANTES tests may administer them to any applicant – or they may administer the tests only to students registered at their institution. Decisions about who will be allowed to test are made by the school. Students should contact the test center to determine current policies and schedules for DANTES testing.

Colleges and universities authorized to administer DANTES tests usually do so throughout the calendar year. Each school sets its own fee for test administration and establishes its own testing schedule. Contact the representative at the administering school directly to make arrangements for testing.

Checklist
For Students

✓ Visit **www.getcollegecredit.com** to obtain a list of tests, fact sheets, test preparation materials, participating colleges and universities, and much more.

✓ Contact your school advisor to confirm that the DSST you selected will fit into your curriculum.

✓ Consult the ***DSST Candidate Information Bulletin*** for answers to specific questions.

✓ Contact the test site to schedule your test.

✓ Prepare for your examination by using the fact sheet as a guide.

✓ Take the test.

If you would like a score report sent to your college or university, it is a good idea to bring the four-digit code with you. You must write the DSST Test Center Code for that institution on your answer sheet at the time of testing. DSST Test Center Codes are noted in the DSST Participating Colleges and Universities listing on the Web site.

If you prefer to send a score report to an institution at a later date, there is a transcript fee of $20 for each transcript ordered.

Thomson Prometric
DSST Program
2000 Lenox Drive, Third Floor
Lawrenceville, NJ 08648

Toll-free: 877-471-9860
609-895-5011

E-mail: pnj-dsst@thomson.com

MAKING A COLLEGE DEGREE WITHIN YOUR REACH

Today, there are many educational alternatives to the classroom—you can learn from your job, your reading, your independent study, and special interests you pursue. You may already have learned the subject matter covered by some college-level courses.

The DSST Program is a nationally recognized testing program that gives you the opportunity to receive college credit for learning acquired outside the traditional college classroom. Colleges and universities throughout the United States administer the program, developed by Thomson Prometric, year-round. Annually, over 90,000 DSSTs are administered to individuals who are interested in continuing their education. Take advantage of the DSST testing program; it speeds the educational process and provides the flexibility adults need, making earning a degree more feasible.

Since requirements differ from college to college, please check with the credit-awarding institution before taking a DSST. More than 1,800 colleges and universities currently award credit for DSSTs, and the number is growing every day. You can choose from 37 test titles in the areas of Social Science, Business, Mathematics, Applied Technology, Humanities, and Physical Science. A brief description of each examination is found on the pages that follow.

Reach Your Career Goals Through DSSTs

Use DSSTs to help you earn your degree, get a promotion, or simply demonstrate that you have college-level knowledge in subjects relevant to your work.

Save Time...

You don't have to sit through classes when you have previously acquired the knowledge or experience for most of what is being taught and can learn the rest yourself. You might be able to bypass introductory-level courses in subject areas you already know.

Save Money...

DSSTs save you money because the classes you bypass by earning credit through the DSST Program are classes you won't have to pay for on your way to earning your degree. You can use the money instead to take more advanced courses that can be more challenging and rewarding.

Improve Your Chances for Admission to College

Each college has its own admission policies; however, having passing scores for DSSTs on your transcript can provide strong evidence of how well you can perform at the college level.

Gain Confidence Performing at a College Level

Many adults returning to college find that lack of confidence is often the greatest hurdle to overcome. Passing a DSST demonstrates your ability to perform on a college level.

Make Up for Courses You May Have Missed

You may be ready to graduate from college and find that you are a few credits short of earning your degree. By using semester breaks, vacation time, or leisure time to study independently, you can prepare to take one or more DSSTs, fulfill your academic requirements, and graduate on time.

If You Cannot Attend Regularly Scheduled Classes...

If your lifestyle or responsibilities prevent you from attending regularly scheduled classes, you can earn your college degree from a college offering an external degree program. The DSST Program allows you to earn your degree by study and experience outside the traditional classroom.

Many colleges and universities offer external degree or distance learning programs. For additional information, contact the college you plan to attend or:

Center for Lifelong Learning
American Council on Education
One DuPont Circle NW, Suite 250
Washington, DC 20036
202-939-9475
www.acenet.edu
(Select "Center for Lifelong Learning" under "Programs & Services" for more information)

Fact Sheets

For each test, there is a Fact Sheet that outlines the topics covered by each test and includes a list of sample questions, a list of recommended references of books that would be useful for review, and the number of credits awarded for a passing score as recommended by the American Council on Education (ACE). *Please note that some schools require scores that are higher than the minimum ACE-recommended passing score.* It is suggested that you check with your college or university to determine what score they require in order to earn credit. You can obtain Fact Sheets by:
- Downloading them from www.getcollegecredit.com
- E-mailing a request to pnj-dsst@thomson.com
- Completing a Candidate Publications Order Form

DSST Online Practice Tests

DSST online practice tests contain items that reflect a *partial range of difficulty* identified in the Content Outline section on each Fact Sheet. There is an online DSST Practice Test in the following categories:
- Mathematics
- Social Science
- Business
- Physical Science
- Applied Technology
- Humanities

Although the online DSST Practice Test questions do not indicate the full range of difficulty you would find in an actual DSST test, they will help you assess your knowledge level. Each online DSST Practice Test can be purchased by visiting www.getcollegecredit.com and clicking on DSST Practice Exams.

TAKING DSST EXAMINATIONS

Earning College Credit for DSST Examinations

To find out if the college of your choice awards credit for passing DSST scores, contact the admissions office or counseling and testing office. The college can also provide information on the scores required for awarding credit, the number of credit hours awarded, and any courses that can be bypassed with satisfactory scores.

It is important that you contact the institution of your choice as early as possible since credit-awarding policies differ among colleges and universities.

Where to Take DSSTs

DSSTs are administered at colleges and universities nationwide. Each location determines the frequency and scheduling of test administrations. To obtain the most current list of participating DSST colleges and universities:

- Visit and download the information from www.getcollegecredit.com
- E-mail pnj-dsst@thomson.com

Scheduling Your Examination

Please be aware that some colleges and universities provide DSST testing services to enrolled students only. After you have selected a college or university that administers DSSTs, you will need to contact them to schedule your test date.

The fee to take a DSST is $60 per test. This fee entitles you to two score reports after the test is scored. One will be sent directly to you and the other will be sent to the college or university that you designate on your answer sheet. You may pay the test fee with a certified check or U.S. money order made payable to Thomson Prometric or you may charge the test fee to your Visa, MasterCard or American Express credit card. Note: The credit card statement will reflect a charge from Thomson Prometric for all DSST examinations. *(Declined credit card charges will be assessed an additional $25 processing fee.)*

In addition, the test site may also require a test administration fee for each examination, to be paid directly to the institution. Contact the test site to determine its administration fee and payment policy.

Other Testing Arrangements

If you are unable to find a participating DSST college or university in your area, you may want to contact the testing office of a local accredited college or university to determine whether a representative from that office will agree to administer the test(s) for you.

The school's representative should then contact the DSST Program at 866-794-3497 to arrange for this administration. If you are unable to locate a test site, contact Thomson Prometric for assistance at pnj-dsst@thomson.com or 866-794-3497.

Testing Accommodations for Students with Disabilities

Thomson Prometric is committed to serving test takers with disabilities by providing services and reasonable testing accommodations as set forth in the provisions of the *Americans with Disabilities Act* (ADA). If you have a disability, as prescribed by the ADA, and require special testing services or arrangements, please contact the test administrator at the test site. You will be asked to submit to the test administrator documentation of your disability and your request for special accommodations. The test administrator will then forward your documentation along with your request for testing accommodations to Thomson Prometric for approval.

Please submit your request as far in advance of your test date as possible so that the necessary accommodations can be made. Only test takers with documented disabilities are eligible for special accommodations.

On the Day of the Examination

It is important to review this information and to have the correct identification present on the day of the examination:
- Arrive on time as a courtesy to the test administrator.
- Bring a valid form of government-issued identification that includes a current photo and your signature (acceptable documents include a driver's license, passport, state-issued identification card or military identification). *Anyone who fails to present valid identification will not be allowed to test.*
- Bring several No. 2 (soft-lead) sharpened pencils with good erasers, a watch, and a black pen if you will be writing an essay.
- Do not bring books or papers.
- Do not bring an alarm watch that beeps, a telephone, or a phone beeper into the testing room.
- The use of nonprogrammable calculators, slide rules, scratch paper and/or other materials is permitted for some of the tests.

DSST SCORING POLICIES

Your DSST examination scores are reported only to you, unless you request that they be sent elsewhere. If you want your scores sent to your college, you must provide the correct DSST code number of the school on your answer sheet at the time you take the test. See the *DSST Directory of Colleges and Universities* on the Web site www.getcollegecredit.com.

If your institution is not listed, contact Thomson Prometric at 866-794-3497 to establish a code number. (Some schools may require a student to be enrolled prior to receiving a score report.)

Receiving Your Score Report

Allow approximately four weeks after testing to receive your score report.

Calling DSST Customer Service before the required four-week score processing time has elapsed will not expedite the processing of your scores. Due to privacy and security requirements, scores will not be reported to students over the telephone under any circumstance.

Scoring of Principles of Public Speaking Speeches

The speech portion of the *Principles of Public Speaking* examination will be sent to speech raters who are faculty members at accredited colleges that currently teach or have previously taught the course. Scores for the *Principles of Public Speaking* examination are available six to eight weeks from receipt by Thomson Prometric. If you take the *Principles of Public Speaking* examination and fail (either the objective, speech portion, or both), you must follow the retesting policy waiting period of six months (180 days) before retaking the entire exam.

Essays

The essays for *Ethics in America* and *Technical Writing* are <u>optional</u> and thus are not scored by raters. The essays are forwarded to the college or university that you designate, along with your score report, for their use in determining the award of credit. <u>Before taking the *Ethics in America* or *Technical Writing* examinations, check with your college or university to determine whether the essay is required.</u>

NOTE: *Principles of Public Speaking* speech topic cassette tapes and essays are kept on file at Thomson Prometric for one year from the date of administration.

How to Get Transcripts

There is a $20 fee for each transcript you request. Payment must be in the form of a certified check, U.S. money order payable to Thomson Prometric, or credit card. Personal checks and debit cards are NOT an acceptable method of payment. One transcript may include scores for one or more examinations taken. To request a transcript, download the Transcript Order Form from www.getcollegecredit.com.

DESCRIPTION OF THE DSST EXAMINATIONS

Mathematics

- **Fundamentals of College Algebra** covers mathematical concepts such as fundamental algebraic operations; linear, absolute value; quadratic equations, inequalities, radials, exponents and logarithms, factoring polynomials and graphing. The use of a nonprogrammable, handheld calculator is permitted.

- **Principles of Statistics** tests the understanding of the various topics of statistics, both qualitatively and quantitatively, and the ability to apply statistical methods to solve a variety of problems. The topics included in this test are descriptive statistics; correlation and regression; probability; chance models and sampling and tests of significance. The use of a nonprogrammable, handheld calculator is permitted.

Social Science

- **Art of the Western World** deals with the history of art during the following periods: classical; Romanesque and Gothic; early Renaissance; high Renaissance, Baroque; rococo; neoclassicism and romanticism; realism, impressionism and post-impressionism; early twentieth century; and post-World War II.

- **Western Europe Since 1945** tests the knowledge of basic facts and terms and the understanding of concepts and principles related to the areas of the historical background of the aftermath of the Second World War and rebuilding of Europe; national political systems; issues and policies in Western European societies; European institutions and processes; and Europe's relations with the rest of the world.

- **An Introduction to the Modern Middle East** emphasizes core knowledge (including geography, Judaism, Christianity, Islam, ethnicity); nineteenth-century European impact; twentieth-century Western influences; World Wars I and II; new nations; social and cultural changes (1900-1960) and the Middle East from 1960 to present.

- **Human/Cultural Geography** includes the Earth and basic facts (coordinate systems, maps, physiography, atmosphere, soils and vegetation, water); culture and environment, spatial processes (social processes, modern economic systems, settlement patterns, political geography); and regional geography.

- **Rise and Fall of the Soviet Union** covers Russia under the Old Regime; the Revolutionary Period; New Economic Policy; Pre-war Stalinism; The Second World War; Post-war Stalinism; The Khrushchev Years; The Brezhnev Era; and reform and collapse.

- **A History of the Vietnam War** covers the history of the roots of the Vietnam War; the First Vietnam War (1946-1954); pre-war developments (1954-1963); American involvement in the Vietnam War; Tet (1968); Vietnamizing the War (1968-1973); Cambodia and Laos; peace; legacies and lessons.

- **The Civil War and Reconstruction** covers the Civil War from presecession (1861) through Reconstruction. It includes causes of the war; secession; Fort Sumter; the war in the east and in the west; major battles; the political situation; assassination of Lincoln; end of the Confederacy; and Reconstruction.

- **Foundations of Education** includes topics such as contemporary issues in education; past and current influences on education (philosophies, democratic ideals, social/economic influences); and the interrelationships between contemporary issues and influences.

- **Life-span Developmental Psychology** covers models and theories; methods of study; ethical issues; biological development; perception, learning and memory; cognition and language; social, emotional, and personality development; social behaviors, family life cycle, extrafamilial settings; singlehood and cohabitation; occupational development and retirement; adjustment to life stresses; and bereavement and loss.

- **Drug and Alcohol Abuse** includes such topics as drug use in society; classification of drugs; pharmacological principles; alcohol (types, effects of, alcoholism); general principles and use of sedative hypnotics, narcotic analgesics, stimulants, and hallucinogens; other drugs (inhalants, steroids); and prevention/treatment.

- **General Anthropology** deals with anthropology as a discipline; theoretical perspectives; physical anthropology; archaeology; social organization; economic organization; political organization; religion; and modernization and application of anthropology.

- **Introduction to Law Enforcement** includes topics such as history and professional movement of law enforcement; overview of the U.S. criminal justice system; police systems in the U.S.; police organization, management, and issues; and U.S. law and precedents.

- **Criminal Justice** deals with criminal behavior (crime in the U.S., theories of crime, types of crime); the criminal justice system (historical origins, legal foundations, due process); police; the court system (history and organization, adult court system, juvenile court, pre-trial and post-trial processes); and corrections.

- **Fundamentals of Counseling** covers historical development (significant influences and people); counselor roles and functions; the counseling relationship; and theoretical approaches to counseling.

Business
- **Principles of Finance** deals with financial statements and planning; time value of money; working capital management; valuation and characteristics; capital budgeting; cost of capital; risk and return; and international financial management. The use of a nonprogrammable, handheld calculator is permitted.

- **Principles of Financial Accounting** includes topics such as general concepts and principles; accounting cycle and classification; transaction analysis; accruals and deferrals; cash and internal control; current accounts; long- and short-term liabilities; capital stock; and financial statements. The use of a nonprogrammable, handheld calculator is permitted.

- **Human Resource Management** covers general employment issues; job analysis; training and development; performance appraisals; compensation issues; security issues; personnel legislation and regulation; labor relations and current issues; an overview of the Human Resource Management Field; Human Resource Planning; Staffing; training and development; compensation issues; safety and health; employee rights and discipline; employment law; labor relations and current issues and trends.

- **Organizational Behavior** deals with the study of organizational behavior (scientific approaches, research designs, data collection methods); individual processes and characteristics; interpersonal and group processes and characteristics; organizational processes and characteristics; and change and development processes.

- **Principles of Supervision** deals with the roles and responsibilities of the supervisor; management functions (planning, organization and staffing, directing at the supervisory level); and other topics (legal issues, stress management, union environments, quality concerns).

- **Business Law II** covers topics such as sales of goods; debtor and creditor relations; business organizations; property; and commercial paper.

- **Introduction to Computing** includes topics such as history and technological generations; hardware/software; applications to information technology; program development; data management; communications and connectivity; and computing and society. The use of a nonprogrammable, handheld calculator is permitted.

- **Management Information Systems** covers systems theory, analysis and design of systems, hardware and software; database management; telecommunications; management of the MIS functional area and informational support.

- **Introduction to Business** deals with economic issues affecting business; international business; government and business; forms of business ownership; small business, entrepreneurship and franchise; management process; human resource management; production and operations; marketing management; financial management; risk management and insurance; and management and information systems.

- **Money and Banking** covers the role and kinds of money; commercial banks and other financial intermediaries; central banking and the Federal Reserve system; money and macroeconomics activity; monetary policy in the U.S.; and the international monetary system.

- **Personal Finance** includes topics such as financial goals and values; budgeting; credit and debt; major purchases; taxes; insurance; investments; and retirement and estate planning. The use of auxiliary materials, such as calculators and slide rules, is NOT permitted.

- **Business Mathematics** deals with basic operations with integers, fractions, and decimals; round numbers; ratios; averages; business graphs; simple interest; compound interest and annuities; net pay and deductions; discounts and markups; depreciation and net worth; corporate securities; distribution of ownership; and stock and asset turnover.

Physical Science

- **Astronomy** covers the history of astronomy, celestial mechanics; celestial systems; astronomical instruments; the solar system; nature and evolution; the galaxy; the universe; determining astronomical distances; and life in the universe.

- **Here's to Your Health** covers mental health and behavior; human development and relationships; substance abuse; fitness and nutrition; risk factors, disease, and disease prevention; and safety, consumer awareness, and environmental concerns.

- **Environment and Humanity** deals with topics such as ecological concepts (ecosystems, global ecology, food chains and webs); environmental impacts; environmental management and conservation; and political processes and the future.

- **Principles of Physical Science I** includes physics: Newton's Laws of Motion; energy and momentum; thermodynamics; wave and optics; electricity and magnetism; chemistry: properties of matter; atomic theory and structure; and chemical reactions.

- **Physical Geology** covers Earth materials; igneous, sedimentary, and metamorphic rocks; surface processes (weathering, groundwater, glaciers, oceanic systems, deserts and winds, hydrologic cycle); internal Earth processes; and applications (mineral and energy resources, environmental geology).

Applied Technology

- **Technical Writing** covers topics such as theory and practice of technical writing; purpose, content, and organizational patterns of common types of technical documents; elements of various technical reports; and technical editing. Students have the option to write a short essay on one of the technical topics provided. Thomson Prometric will not score the essay; however, for determining the award of credit, a copy of the essay will be forwarded to the college or university you've designated along with the score report or transcript.

Humanities

- **Ethics in America** deals with ethical traditions (Greek views, Biblical traditions, moral law, consequential ethics, feminist ethics); ethical analysis of issues arising in interpersonal and personal-societal relationships and in professional and occupational roles; and relationships between ethical traditions and the ethical analysis of situations. Students have the option to write an essay to analyze a morally problematic situation in terms of issues relevant to a decision and arguments for alternative positions. Thomson Prometric will not score the essay; however, for determining the award of credit, a copy of the essay will be forwarded to the college or university you've designated along with the score report or transcript.

- **Introduction to World Religions** covers topics such as dimensions and approaches to religion; primal religions; Hinduism; Buddhism; Confucianism; Taoism; Judaism; Christianity; and Islam.

- **Principles of Public Speaking** consists of two parts: Part One consists of multiple-choice questions covering considerations of Principles of Public Speaking; audience analysis; purposes of speeches; structure/organization; content/supporting materials; research; language and style; delivery; communication apprehension; listening and feedback; and criticism and evaluation. Part Two requires the student to record an impromptu persuasive speech that will be scored.

FREQUENTLY ASKED QUESTIONS ABOUT DSSTs

In order to pass the test, must I study from one of the recommended references?

The recommended references are a listing of books that were being used as textbooks in college courses of the same or similar title at the time the test was developed. Appropriate textbooks for study are not limited to those listed in the fact sheet. If you wish to obtain study resources to prepare for the examination, you may reference either the current edition of the listed titles or textbooks currently used at a local college or university for the same class title. It is recommended that you reference more than one textbook on the topics outlined in the fact sheet. You should begin by checking textbook content against the content outline included on the front page of the DSST fact sheet before selecting textbooks that cover the text content from which to study. Textbooks may be found at the campus bookstore of a local college or university offering a course on the subject.

Is there a penalty for guessing on the tests?

There is no penalty for guessing on DSSTs, so you should mark an answer for each question.

How much time will I have to complete the test?

Many DSSTs can be completed within 90 minutes; however, additional time can be allowed if necessary.

What should I do if I find a test question irregularity?

Continue testing and then report the irregularity to the test administrator after the test. This may be done by asking that the test administrator note the irregularity on the Supervisor's Irregularity Report or you can write to Thomson Prometric, DSST Program, 2000 Lenox Drive, Third Floor, Lawrenceville, NJ 08648, and indicate the form and question number(s) or circumstances as well as your name and address.

When will I receive my score report?

Allow approximately four weeks from the date of testing to receive your score report. Allow six to eight weeks to receive a score report for the *Principles of Public Speaking* examination.

Will my test scores be released without my permission?

Your test score will not be released to anyone other than the school you designate on your answer sheet unless you write to us and ask us to send a transcript elsewhere. Instructions about how to do this can be found on your score report. Your scores may be used for research purposes, but individual scores are never made public nor are individuals identified if research findings are made public.

If I do not achieve a passing score on the test, how long must I wait until I can take the test again?

If you do not receive a score on the test that will enable you to obtain credit for the course, you may take the test again after six months (180 days). Please do not attempt to take the test before six months (180 days) have passed because you will receive a score report marked <u>*invalid*</u> and your test fee will not be refunded.

Can my test scores be canceled?

The test administrator is required to report any irregularities to Thomson Prometric. <u>The consequence of bringing unauthorized materials into the testing room, or giving or receiving help, will be the forfeiture of your test fee and the invalidation of test scores.</u> The DSST Program reserves the right to cancel scores and not issue score reports in such situations.

What can I do if I feel that my test scores were not accurately reported?

Thomson Prometric recognizes the extreme importance of test results to candidates and has a multi-step quality-control procedure to help ensure that reported scores are accurate. If you have reason to believe that your score(s) were not accurately reported, you may request to have your answer sheet reviewed and hand scored.

The fees for this service are:
- $20 fee if requested within six months of the test date
- $30 fee if requested more than six months from the test date
- $30 fee if a re-evaluation of the *Principles of Public Speaking* speech is requested

The fee for this service can be paid by credit card or by certified check or U.S. money order payable to Thomson Prometric. Submit your request for score verification along with the appropriate fee or credit card information (credit card number and expiration date) to Thomson Prometric, DSST Program, 2000 Lenox Drive, Third Floor, Lawrenceville, NJ 08648. Include your full name, the test title, the date you took the test, and your Social Security number. Candidates will be notified if a scoring discrepancy is discovered within four weeks of receipt of the request.

What does ACE recommendation mean?

The ACE recommendation is the minimum passing score recommended by the American Council on Education for any given test. It is equivalent to the average score of students in the DSST norming sample who received a grade of C for the course. Some schools require a score higher than the ACE recommendation.

Who is NLC?

National Learning Corporation (NLC) has been successfully preparing candidates for 40 years for over 5,000 exams. NLC publishes Passbook® study guides to help candidates prepare for all DANTES and CLEP exams and almost every other type of exam from high school through adult career.

Go to our website — www.passbooks.com — or call (800) 632-8888 for information about ordering our Passbooks.

To get detailed information on the DSST program and DSST preparation materials, visit www.getcollegecredit.com.

If you are interested in taking the DSST exams, call 877-471-9860 or e-mail pnj-dsst@thomson.com.

DSST® THE CIVIL WAR AND RECONSTRUCTION

EXAM INFORMATION
This exam was developed to enable schools to award credit to students for knowledge equivalent to that learned by students taking the course. This examination includes the Civil War from pre-secession (1861) through Reconstruction. Includes causes of the war; secession; Fort Sumter; major battles; the political situation; assassination of Lincoln; end of the Confederacy; and Reconstruction.

The exam contains 100 questions to be answered in 2 hours.

EXAM CONTENT OUTLINE
The following is an outline of the content areas covered in the examination. The approximate percentage of the examination devoted to each content area is also noted.

I. **Causes of the War – 16%**
   a. United States Society in the Mid-Nineteenth Century
      1. Industrialization
      2. Religiosity
      3. Standard of living
      4. Demographics
   b. Slavery
   c. Anti-Slavery and Abolition movement
   d. Westward Expansion of Free and Slave Territory
      1. Missouri Compromise
      2. Mexican War
      3. Compromise of 1850
      4. Kansas - Nebraska Act
      5. Birth of Republican Party
      6. Bleeding Kansas
      7. Dred Scott decision
   e. John Brown's raid on Harper's Ferry
   f. Political situation in 1860

II. **1861 – 11%**
   a. Secession
   b. Formation of Confederacy
   c. Fort Sumter
   d. Lincoln's Call for Volunteers
   e. First Manassas (Bull Run)
   f. Union Army versus Confederate Army
   g. Lincoln versus Davis leadership

III. **1862 – 17%**
   a. Southern Strategy
   b. War in the East
   c. War in the West
   d. Major Battles
   e. Emancipation proclamation

IV. **1863 – 19%**
   a. Casualties
   b. Role of women in the War
   c. Black Americans and the War
   d. Major Battles

V. **1864 – 15%**
   a. Political situation
      1. Northern demoralization
      2. Presidential election in north
      3. South cut in half and isolated
   b. War in the West
      1. Capture of Atlanta
      2. Sherman's march to the sea and total war
   c. War in the East
      1. Grant and the Army of the Potomac
      2. Lee and the Army of northern Virginia
      3. Major battles- the rise of modern warfare

VI. **1865 - 7%**
   a. Sherman's Carolina Campaign
   b. Fall of Richmond
   c. Lee's Surrender
   d. Assassination of Lincoln
   e. End of the Confederacy
   f. Cost of the War

VII. **Reconstruction - 15%**
   a. Presidential Reconstruction Plans
   b. Southern Response
   c. Congressional Reconstruction Plans
      1. Radical Republicans
      2. Reconstruction acts
      3. Thirteenth, Fourteenth and Fifteenth Amendments
      4. Impeachment
      5. Freedmen's Bureau
      6. Civil Rights Act
   d. Military Reconstruction
      1. Response to Johnson's policies
      2. Elected black office-holders
      3. Scalawags and carpet-baggers
      4. Secret terrorist societies
   e. End of Reconstruction

REFERENCES
Below is a list of reference publications that were either used as a reference to create the exam, or were used as textbooks in college courses of the same or similar title at the time the test was developed. You

may reference either the current edition of these titles **or** textbooks currently used at a local college or university for the same class title. It is recommended that you reference **more than one textbook** on the topics outlined in this fact sheet.

You should **begin by checking textbook content against the content outline** provided **before** selecting textbooks that cover the test content from which to study.

Sources for study material are suggested but not limited to the following:

1. Foner, Eric (2011). *Reconstruction: America's Unfinished Revolution, 1863-1877.* New York, NY: Harper and Row, current edition.

2. Goodwin, Doris Kearns (2005). *Team of Rivals: The Political Genius of Abraham Lincoln.* Current edition.

3. McPherson, James (1988). *Battle Cry of Freedom: The Civil War Era.* New York, NY: Oxford University Press, current edition.

4. McPherson, James & Hogue, James K. (2010). *Ordeal by Fire: The Civil War and Reconstruction.* New York, NY: McGraw-Hill, 4th Ed.

SAMPLE QUESTIONS

All test questions are in a multiple-choice format, with one correct answer and three incorrect options. These are samples of the types of questions that may appear on the exam.

1. The last major Confederate stronghold on the Mississippi River was
   a. Memphis
   b. Vicksburg
   c. New Orleans
   d. Fort Donnellson

2. Under the fourteenth amendment, many of those who had served in the Confederate government or army were
   a. automatically reinstated as full citizens of the United States
   b. forbidden to bear arms
   c. forbidden to hold public office
   d. interned for a minimum of six months

3. The Union general in command of the Shenandoah Valley campaigns of 1864 was
   a. Philip Kearny
   b. Philip Sheridan
   c. William T. Sherman
   d. George A. Custer

4. When the southern states began to secede, Kentucky's response was
   a. enthusiastic support for the south, followed by Kentucky's secession
   b. reluctant support for the south, followed by Kentucky's secession
   c. a declaration of neutrality, followed by a gradual shift to Unionism
   d. a firm resolve to remain in the Union, followed by an enthusiastic response to Lincoln's call for troops

5. Of those who died as a result of the war, the majority were
   a. civilians deliberately or accidentally killed by hostile troops
   b. soldiers killed outright in combat
   c. soldiers who died later of wounds received in battle
   d. soldiers who died of disease

6. Prior to his attack on Harper's Ferry, John Brown was a
   a. free-state agitator in Kansas
   b. publisher of a leading abolitionist newspaper
   c. slave owner in Missouri
   d. station owner on the underground railroad

7. The South's naval strategy was to use its
   a. large navy to attack northern ports and bring the war to the north
   b. large navy to defend its ports and prevent a Union blockade
   c. relatively small navy to protect its ports and keep them open for blockade runners
   d. relatively small navy to convoy supply ships from Europe and South America

8. Which of the following nearly caused the outbreak of hostilities between the United States and Great Britain?
   a. Britain's willingness to receive the Confederate cruiser *Alabama* in its ports
   b. British gunrunning to the Confederate states through the union blockade
   c. British reactions to Lincoln's Emancipation Proclamation
   d. British objections to the seizure of two confederate diplomats traveling on a British ship

9. Grant's confrontation with Lee at Petersburg can best be described as a
   a. confederate rout of the union army
   b. swift, decisive victory for the union army

c. tragic blunder on the part of the union high command
   d. prolonged siege ending in union victory

10. Through the course of the Civil War, which of the following was true of Jefferson Davis's cabinet?
    a. It remained stable in makeup and firm in support of the president
    b. It remained stable in makeup but opposed to the president on many issues
    c. Its members changed considerably but remained constant in support for the president
    d. Its members changed considerably and were divided in their support for the president

11. Which of the following correctly states a major difference between the population of the North and South at the middle of the 19th century?
    a. In the north, the vast majority of the adult white population was literate, while in the south less than half the adult white population could read and write
    b. In the south, people were much more religious than people in the north, attended church more frequently, and often participated in religious reawakening
    c. In the north, the white population included large numbers of immigrants, while in the south the white population was largely of British descent
    d. In the south, a larger proportion of the white population had traveled extensively within the region, while the northern white population remained familiar only with the area in which they were born

12. Which of the following is a true statement about the Union presidential election of 1864?
    a. It was the first presidential election ever held by a nation involved in a civil war
    b. It attracted little public interest because the people of the north were occupied with the war effort
    c. Lincoln's reelection was considered a certainty because the nation did not want to change governments in the middle of the war
    d. Lincoln's reelection was considered unlikely because Lincoln had failed to support abolition prior to the war

CREDIT RECOMMENDATIONS

The American Council on Education's College Credit Recommendation Service (ACE CREDIT) has evaluated the DSST test development process and content of this exam. It has made the following recommendations:

Area or Course Equivalent	The Civil War and Reconstruction
Level	Upper-level baccalaureate
Amount of Credit	Three (3) semester hours
Minimum Score	400
Source	American Council on Education – College Credit Recommendation Service

Answers to sample questions: 1-B; 2-C; 3-B; 4-C; 5-D; 6-A; 7-C; 8-D; 9-D; 10-D; 11-C; 12-A.

HOW TO TAKE A TEST

You have studied long, hard and conscientiously.

With your official admission card in hand, and your heart pounding, you have been admitted to the examination room.

You note that there are several hundred other applicants in the examination room waiting to take the same test.

They all appear to be equally well prepared.

You know that nothing but your best effort will suffice. The "moment of truth" is at hand: you now have to demonstrate objectively, in writing, your knowledge of content and your understanding of subject matter.

You are fighting the most important battle of your life—to pass and/or score high on an examination which will determine your career and provide the economic basis for your livelihood.

What extra, special things should you know and should you do in taking the examination?

I. YOU MUST PASS AN EXAMINATION

A. WHAT EVERY CANDIDATE SHOULD KNOW
Examination applicants often ask us for help in preparing for the written test. What can I study in advance? What kinds of questions will be asked? How will the test be given? How will the papers be graded?

B. HOW ARE EXAMS DEVELOPED?
Examinations are carefully written by trained technicians who are specialists in the field known as "psychological measurement," in consultation with recognized authorities in the field of work that the test will cover. These experts recommend the subject matter areas or skills to be tested; only those knowledges or skills important to your success on the job are included. The most reliable books and source materials available are used as references. Together, the experts and technicians judge the difficulty level of the questions.
Test technicians know how to phrase questions so that the problem is clearly stated. Their ethics do not permit "trick" or "catch" questions. Questions may have been tried out on sample groups, or subjected to statistical analysis, to determine their usefulness.
Written tests are often used in combination with performance tests, ratings of training and experience, and oral interviews. All of these measures combine to form the best-known means of finding the right person for the right job.

II. HOW TO PASS THE WRITTEN TEST

A. BASIC STEPS

1) Study the announcement

How, then, can you know what subjects to study? Our best answer is: "Learn as much as possible about the class of positions for which you've applied." The exam will test the knowledge, skills and abilities needed to do the work.

Your most valuable source of information about the position you want is the official exam announcement. This announcement lists the training and experience qualifications. Check these standards and apply only if you come reasonably close to meeting them. Many jurisdictions preview the written test in the exam announcement by including a section called "Knowledge and Abilities Required," "Scope of the Examination," or some similar heading. Here you will find out specifically what fields will be tested.

2) Choose appropriate study materials

If the position for which you are applying is technical or advanced, you will read more advanced, specialized material. If you are already familiar with the basic principles of your field, elementary textbooks would waste your time. Concentrate on advanced textbooks and technical periodicals. Think through the concepts and review difficult problems in your field.

These are all general sources. You can get more ideas on your own initiative, following these leads. For example, training manuals and publications of the government agency which employs workers in your field can be useful, particularly for technical and professional positions. A letter or visit to the government department involved may result in more specific study suggestions, and certainly will provide you with a more definite idea of the exact nature of the position you are seeking.

3) Study this book!

III. KINDS OF TESTS

Tests are used for purposes other than measuring knowledge and ability to perform specified duties. For some positions, it is equally important to test ability to make adjustments to new situations or to profit from training. In others, basic mental abilities not dependent on information are essential. Questions which test these things may not appear as pertinent to the duties of the position as those which test for knowledge and information. Yet they are often highly important parts of a fair examination. For very general questions, it is almost impossible to help you direct your study efforts. What we can do is to point out some of the more common of these general abilities needed in public service positions and describe some typical questions.

1) General information

Broad, general information has been found useful for predicting job success in some kinds of work. This is tested in a variety of ways, from vocabulary lists to questions about current events. Basic background in some field of work, such as sociology or economics, may be sampled in a group of questions. Often these are principles which have become familiar to most persons through exposure rather than through formal training. It is difficult to advise you how to study for these questions; being alert to the world around you is our best suggestion.

2) Verbal ability

An example of an ability needed in many positions is verbal or language ability. Verbal ability is, in brief, the ability to use and understand words. Vocabulary and grammar tests are typical measures of this ability. Reading comprehension or paragraph interpretation questions are common in many kinds of civil service tests. You are given a paragraph of written material and asked to find its central meaning.

IV. KINDS OF QUESTIONS

1. Multiple-choice Questions

Most popular of the short-answer questions is the "multiple choice" or "best answer" question. It can be used, for example, to test for factual knowledge, ability to solve problems or judgment in meeting situations found at work.

A multiple-choice question is normally one of three types:
- It can begin with an incomplete statement followed by several possible endings. You are to find the one ending which best completes the statement, although some of the others may not be entirely wrong.
- It can also be a complete statement in the form of a question which is answered by choosing one of the statements listed.
- It can be in the form of a problem – again you select the best answer.

Here is an example of a multiple-choice question with a discussion which should give you some clues as to the method for choosing the right answer:

When an employee has a complaint about his assignment, the action which will best help him overcome his difficulty is to
    A. discuss his difficulty with his coworkers
    B. take the problem to the head of the organization
    C. take the problem to the person who gave him the assignment
    D. say nothing to anyone about his complaint

In answering this question, you should study each of the choices to find which is best. Consider choice "A" – Certainly an employee may discuss his complaint with fellow employees, but no change or improvement can result, and the complaint remains unresolved. Choice "B" is a poor choice since the head of the organization probably does not know what assignment you have been given, and taking your problem to him is known as "going over the head" of the supervisor. The supervisor, or person who made the assignment, is the person who can clarify it or correct any injustice. Choice "C" is, therefore, correct. To say nothing, as in choice "D," is unwise. Supervisors have and interest in knowing the problems employees are facing, and the employee is seeking a solution to his problem.

2. True/False

3. Matching Questions

Matching an answer from a column of choices within another column.

V. RECORDING YOUR ANSWERS

Computer terminals are used more and more today for many different kinds of exams.

For an examination with very few applicants, you may be told to record your answers in the test booklet itself. Separate answer sheets are much more common. If this separate answer sheet is to be scored by machine – and this is often the case – it is highly important that you mark your answers correctly in order to get credit.

VI. BEFORE THE TEST

YOUR PHYSICAL CONDITION IS IMPORTANT

If you are not well, you can't do your best work on tests. If you are half asleep, you can't do your best either. Here are some tips:

1) Get about the same amount of sleep you usually get. Don't stay up all night before the test, either partying or worrying—DON'T DO IT!
2) If you wear glasses, be sure to wear them when you go to take the test. This goes for hearing aids, too.
3) If you have any physical problems that may keep you from doing your best, be sure to tell the person giving the test. If you are sick or in poor health, you relay cannot do your best on any test. You can always come back and take the test some other time.

Common sense will help you find procedures to follow to get ready for an examination. Too many of us, however, overlook these sensible measures. Indeed, nervousness and fatigue have been found to be the most serious reasons why applicants fail to do their best on civil service tests. Here is a list of reminders:

- Begin your preparation early – Don't wait until the last minute to go scurrying around for books and materials or to find out what the position is all about.
- Prepare continuously – An hour a night for a week is better than an all-night cram session. This has been definitely established. What is more, a night a week for a month will return better dividends than crowding your study into a shorter period of time.
- Locate the place of the exam – You have been sent a notice telling you when and where to report for the examination. If the location is in a different town or otherwise unfamiliar to you, it would be well to inquire the best route and learn something about the building.
- Relax the night before the test – Allow your mind to rest. Do not study at all that night. Plan some mild recreation or diversion; then go to bed early and get a good night's sleep.
- Get up early enough to make a leisurely trip to the place for the test – This way unforeseen events, traffic snarls, unfamiliar buildings, etc. will not upset you.
- Dress comfortably – A written test is not a fashion show. You will be known by number and not by name, so wear something comfortable.
- Leave excess paraphernalia at home – Shopping bags and odd bundles will get in your way. You need bring only the items mentioned in the official notice you received; usually everything you need is provided. Do not bring reference books to the exam. They will only confuse those last minutes and be taken away from you when in the test room.

- Arrive somewhat ahead of time – If because of transportation schedules you must get there very early, bring a newspaper or magazine to take your mind off yourself while waiting.
- Locate the examination room – When you have found the proper room, you will be directed to the seat or part of the room where you will sit. Sometimes you are given a sheet of instructions to read while you are waiting. Do not fill out any forms until you are told to do so; just read them and be prepared.
- Relax and prepare to listen to the instructions
- If you have any physical problem that may keep you from doing your best, be sure to tell the test administrator. If you are sick or in poor health, you really cannot do your best on the exam. You can come back and take the test some other time.

VII. AT THE TEST

The day of the test is here and you have the test booklet in your hand. The temptation to get going is very strong. Caution! There is more to success than knowing the right answers. You must know how to identify your papers and understand variations in the type of short-answer question used in this particular examination. Follow these suggestions for maximum results from your efforts:

1) Cooperate with the monitor

The test administrator has a duty to create a situation in which you can be as much at ease as possible. He will give instructions, tell you when to begin, check to see that you are marking your answer sheet correctly, and so on. He is not there to guard you, although he will see that your competitors do not take unfair advantage. He wants to help you do your best.

2) Listen to all instructions

Don't jump the gun! Wait until you understand all directions. In most civil service tests you get more time than you need to answer the questions. So don't be in a hurry. Read each word of instructions until you clearly understand the meaning. Study the examples, listen to all announcements and follow directions. Ask questions if you do not understand what to do.

3) Identify your papers

Civil service exams are usually identified by number only. You will be assigned a number; you must not put your name on your test papers. Be sure to copy your number correctly. Since more than one exam may be given, copy your exact examination title.

4) Plan your time

Unless you are told that a test is a "speed" or "rate of work" test, speed itself is usually not important. Time enough to answer all the questions will be provided, but this does not mean that you have all day. An overall time limit has been set. Divide the total time (in minutes) by the number of questions to determine the approximate time you have for each question.

5) Do not linger over difficult questions

If you come across a difficult question, mark it with a paper clip (useful to have along) and come back to it when you have been through the booklet. One caution if you do this – be sure to skip a number on your answer sheet as well. Check often to be sure that you have not lost your place and that you are marking in the row numbered the same as the question you are answering.

6) Read the questions

Be sure you know what the question asks! Many capable people are unsuccessful because they failed to read the questions correctly.

7) Answer all questions

Unless you have been instructed that a penalty will be deducted for incorrect answers, it is better to guess than to omit a question.

8) Speed tests

It is often better NOT to guess on speed tests. It has been found that on timed tests people are tempted to spend the last few seconds before time is called in marking answers at random – without even reading them – in the hope of picking up a few extra points. To discourage this practice, the instructions may warn you that your score will be "corrected" for guessing. That is, a penalty will be applied. The incorrect answers will be deducted from the correct ones, or some other penalty formula will be used.

9) Review your answers

If you finish before time is called, go back to the questions you guessed or omitted to give them further thought. Review other answers if you have time.

10) Return your test materials

If you are ready to leave before others have finished or time is called, take ALL your materials to the monitor and leave quietly. Never take any test material with you. The monitor can discover whose papers are not complete, and taking a test booklet may be grounds for disqualification.

VIII. EXAMINATION TECHNIQUES

1) Read the general instructions carefully. These are usually printed on the first page of the exam booklet. As a rule, these instructions refer to the timing of the examination; the fact that you should not start work until the signal and must stop work at a signal, etc. If there are any special instructions, such as a choice of questions to be answered, make sure that you note this instruction carefully.

2) When you are ready to start work on the examination, that is as soon as the signal has been given, read the instructions to each question booklet, underline any key words or phrases, such as least, best, outline, describe and the like. In this way you will tend to answer as requested rather than discover on reviewing your paper that you listed without describing, that you selected the worst choice rather than the best choice, etc.

3) If the examination is of the objective or multiple-choice type – that is, each question will also give a series of possible answers: A, B, C or D, and you are called upon to select the best answer and write the letter next to that answer on your answer paper – it is advisable to start answering each question in turn. There may be anywhere from 50 to 100 such questions in the three or four hours allotted and you can see how much time would be taken if you read through all the questions before beginning to answer any. Furthermore, if you

come across a question or group of questions which you know would be difficult to answer, it would undoubtedly affect your handling of all the other questions.

4) If the examination is of the essay type and contains but a few questions, it is a moot point as to whether you should read all the questions before starting to answer any one. Of course, if you are given a choice – say five out of seven and the like – then it is essential to read all the questions so you can eliminate the two that are most difficult. If, however, you are asked to answer all the questions, there may be danger in trying to answer the easiest one first because you may find that you will spend too much time on it. The best technique is to answer the first question, then proceed to the second, etc.

5) Time your answers. Before the exam begins, write down the time it started, then add the time allowed for the examination and write down the time it must be completed, then divide the time available somewhat as follows:
   - If 3-1/2 hours are allowed, that would be 210 minutes. If you have 80 objective-type questions, that would be an average of 2-1/2 minutes per question. Allow yourself no more than 2 minutes per question, or a total of 160 minutes, which will permit about 50 minutes to review.
   - If for the time allotment of 210 minutes there are 7 essay questions to answer, that would average about 30 minutes a question. Give yourself only 25 minutes per question so that you have about 35 minutes to review.

6) The most important instruction is to read each question and make sure you know what is wanted. The second most important instruction is to time yourself properly so that you answer every question. The third most important instruction is to answer every question. Guess if you have to but include something for each question. Remember that you will receive no credit for a blank and will probably receive some credit if you write something in answer to an essay question. If you guess a letter – say "B" for a multiple-choice question – you may have guessed right. If you leave a blank as an answer to a multiple-choice question, the examiners may respect your feelings but it will not add a point to your score. Some exams may penalize you for wrong answers, so in such cases only, you may not want to guess unless you have some basis for your answer.

7) Suggestions
   a. Objective-type questions
      1. Examine the question booklet for proper sequence of pages and questions
      2. Read all instructions carefully
      3. Skip any question which seems too difficult; return to it after all other questions have been answered
      4. Apportion your time properly; do not spend too much time on any single question or group of questions
      5. Note and underline key words – all, most, fewest, least, best, worst, same, opposite, etc.
      6. Pay particular attention to negatives
      7. Note unusual option, e.g., unduly long, short, complex, different or similar in content to the body of the question
      8. Observe the use of "hedging" words – probably, may, most likely, etc.

9. Make sure that your answer is put next to the same number as the question
10. Do not second-guess unless you have good reason to believe the second answer is definitely more correct
11. Cross out original answer if you decide another answer is more accurate; do not erase until you are ready to hand your paper in
12. Answer all questions; guess unless instructed otherwise
13. Leave time for review

  b. Essay questions
1. Read each question carefully
2. Determine exactly what is wanted. Underline key words or phrases.
3. Decide on outline or paragraph answer
4. Include many different points and elements unless asked to develop any one or two points or elements
5. Show impartiality by giving pros and cons unless directed to select one side only
6. Make and write down any assumptions you find necessary to answer the questions
7. Watch your English, grammar, punctuation and choice of words
8. Time your answers; don't crowd material

8) Answering the essay question

Most essay questions can be answered by framing the specific response around several key words or ideas. Here are a few such key words or ideas:

M's: manpower, materials, methods, money, management
P's: purpose, program, policy, plan, procedure, practice, problems, pitfalls, personnel, public relations

  a. Six basic steps in handling problems:
1. Preliminary plan and background development
2. Collect information, data and facts
3. Analyze and interpret information, data and facts
4. Analyze and develop solutions as well as make recommendations
5. Prepare report and sell recommendations
6. Install recommendations and follow up effectiveness

  b. Pitfalls to avoid
1. Taking things for granted – A statement of the situation does not necessarily imply that each of the elements is necessarily true; for example, a complaint may be invalid and biased so that all that can be taken for granted is that a complaint has been registered
2. Considering only one side of a situation – Wherever possible, indicate several alternatives and then point out the reasons you selected the best one
3. Failing to indicate follow up – Whenever your answer indicates action on your part, make certain that you will take proper follow-up action to see how successful your recommendations, procedures or actions turn out to be
4. Taking too long in answering any single question – Remember to time your answers properly

EXAMINATION SECTION

EXAMINATION SECTION
TEST 1

DIRECTIONS: Each question or incomplete statement is followed by several suggested answers or completions. Select the one that BEST answers the question or completes the statement. *PRINT THE LETTER OF THE CORRECT ANSWER IN THE SPACE AT THE RIGHT.*

1. Which of the following Midwestern states was considered to be the heart of *Copperhead country* during the latter years of the Civil War?   1._____

    A. Missouri
    B. Ohio
    C. Minnesota
    D. Iowa

2. Throughout the War, the Cabinet members with whom President Lincoln worked most closely were   2._____

    A. Edward Bates and Edwin M. Stanton
    B. Edwin M. Stanton and William H. Seward
    C. Gideon Welles and Simon Cameron
    D. William H. Seward and Salmon P. Chase

3. Each of the following was an element of the Wade-Davis reconstruction bill passed by the Republicans in 1864 EXCEPT   3._____

    A. restoration to the Union contingent upon an oath of allegiance from 50 percent of voters in a state
    B. permission of suffrage for all whites who took an oath of future loyalty
    C. the mandated election of delegates to a constitutional convention
    D. specific legal safeguards for the liberty of freedmen

4. Which of the following was NOT a *border* state during the Civil War conflict?   4._____

    A. Virginia   B. Missouri   C. Maryland   D. Kentucky

5. Which of the following was not a significant problem associated with the practice of *paroling* prisoners of war during the Civil War?   5._____

    A. Paroled prisoners expected to be sent home.
    B. Most paroled prisoners would simply return to active duty.
    C. Order in parole camps was difficult to maintain.
    D. It encouraged some soldiers to fall into the hands of the enemy.

6. The battle of Antietam is generally considered in hindsight to have been a   6._____

    A. total victory for the Union forces
    B. tactical victory for the Confederacy
    C. tactical draw, but a strategic defeat for the Confederacy
    D. tactical draw, but a strategic defeat for the Union

7. In 1864, the greatest threat to the military strength of the Union was the   7._____

    A. rising tide of Copperhead sentiment throughout the Midwest
    B. high rate of desertion
    C. enormous casualty rate of Grant's Virginia campaigns
    D. end of the three-year enlistments that composed roughly half of Union forces

8. Confederates justified secession in 1860-1861 based upon the
   A. writ of *habeas corpus*
   B. preamble of the Constitution
   C. slave tariff
   D. supreme-law clause of the Constitution

9. Which of the following states refused to ratify the 13th Amendment to the Constitution in 1864?
   A. Missouri   B. Tennessee   C. Kentucky   D. Louisiana

10. Two days after his signing of the preliminary Emancipation Proclamation, which of the following edicts was added by President Lincoln?
    The
    A. suspension of the writ of habeas corpus in certain regions
    B. justification of emancipation on military grounds
    C. suspension of the Atlantic slave trade
    D. endorsement of voluntary colonization of freed slaves

11. As the Southern states began to secede from the Union in 1861, the initial strategic response on the part of most Republicans was to
    A. capitulate on the question of the slave trade
    B. reinforce all government and military installations that had not yet been seized
    C. sit tight and do nothing to encourage secessionists or to alienate Southern Unionists
    D. retake government and military installations that had been seized

12. The strongest defensive works of the war were constructed at
    A. Vicksburg   B. Chancellorsville
    C. Gettysburg   D. Appomattox

13. Upon taking command of the Union's Army of the Potomac in 1861, Gen. George McClellan initially succeeded in
    A. replacing most regimental and company officers
    B. instilling lost pride and discipline
    C. winning new recruits to the Union cause
    D. launching a successful offensive into Confederate territory

14. While terrorist groups such as the Ku Klux Klan grew stronger and bolder in the South during 1868, federal troops were generally ineffective in dealing with the new wave of violence, primarily because
    A. membership in these groups was too large for them to be stopped
    B. martial law was now impossible in newly reconstructed states
    C. federal troops were generally held in check by President Johnson
    D. such groups enjoyed broad-based popular support

15. In the agricultural system that existed in the South prior to the war, a *factor* or commission merchant served each of the following purposes EXCEPT

   A. advancing credit to the planter
   B. directly purchasing crops in times of surplus
   C. taking charge of the planter's crop when it reached an urban center
   D. serving as the planter's purchasing agent to obtain consumer goods

16. Approximately what percentage of Union soldiers who fought in the war were conscripts?

   A. 10   B. 25   C. 40   D. 55

17. President Lincoln's _____ effectively constituted the declaration of war that began the Civil War conflict.

   A. ordering of a naval blockade of the South
   B. expansion of regular army and naval forces beyond the number authorized by law
   C. issuance of the Emancipation Proclamation
   D. suspension of the writ of *habeas corpus* in parts of the country

18. Which of the following states adopted black suffrage by referendum in 1868?

   A. Arkansas   B. Wisconsin   C. Iowa   D. Missouri

19. Approximately what percentage of Civil War battle casalties were infantry soldiers?

   A. 25-35   B. 45-55   C. 60-70   D. 80-90

20. The PRIMARY reason for the overcrowding of Confederate prisons with Union soldiers in 1864 was the

   A. Confederate desire to inflict suffering on Union soldiers
   B. breakdown of the prisoner exchange program
   C. lack of Confederate resources for building and maintaining prison facilities
   D. lack of officers willing to oversee military prisons

21. The clearest explanation for why President Lincoln did not proclaim the war to be fought for the freedom of slaves, as well as for the preservation of the Union, was that he

   A. wanted to retain the favor of European governments
   B. still considered himself bound by the constitutional guarantee of slavery in the states
   C. was personally sympathetic to the cause of slavery
   D. wanted to retain the allegiance of Northern Democrats

22. Which Union general led the victory at Gettysburg?

   A. William S. Rosecrans   B. George Armstrong Custer
   C. Joseph Hooker   D. George Gordon Meade

23. During the period of modernization that occurred in the United States economy, the first and probably most important changes came in the sector of

   A. communications   B. agriculture
   C. steel production   D. transportation

24. Each of the following states abolished slavery before the end of the war EXCEPT

    A. Arkansas   B. Delaware   C. Louisiana   D. Maryland

25. During the first two years of the war, European liberals became increasingly disillusioned with the Union cause, mostly because

    A. President Lincoln had frequently overstepped the authority of his office in the prosecution of the war and civil liberties had been widely violated
    B. Union soldiers were pillaging and confiscating Southern property on their campaigns
    C. the war was ostensibly being fought to restore a slaveholding Union
    D. the writ of *habeas corpus* had been suspended in certain regions

26. The first year that blacks were allowed in congressional galleries in the United States was

    A. 1860   B. 1862   C. 1864   D. 1866

27. The _____ was NOT mentioned in the platform developed at the 1864 Democratic Convention in Chicago.

    A. restoration of the writ of *habeas corpus*
    B. recognition of the states' rights to practice slavery
    C. immediate end of the war
    D. restoration of the Union as a condition for peace

28. Approximately how many Union soldiers lost their lives in the war?

    A. 120,000   B. 250,000   C. 360,000   D. 430,000

29. At the start of the Civil War, the manpower pool of the South was approximately _____ that of the North's.

    A. one-eighth   B. one-third
    C. three-quarters   D. the same as

30. The movement to impeach President Johnson, stoked by Republicans, was finally accomplished on the grounds that

    A. the President was guilty of conduct that was harmful to the public
    B. the President had violated the Tenure of Office Act by suspending a Cabinet member without congressional approval
    C. the President had criminally conspired with ex-Confederate officials to affect the fall of several Southern Republican regimes
    D. President Johnson had committed a grave misuse of his executive powers

31. Which of the following offers the best explanation for the Union defeat at the second Battle of Bull Run in the summer of 1862?

    A. A lack of coordination due to tensions between the Union commanders, Generals Pope and McClellan
    B. Inferior Union intelligence about the location and strength of Confederate troops
    C. The military brilliance of Robert E. Lee and Stonewall Jackson
    D. The better-trained and more disciplined Confederate infantry

32. During the 1830s, the *Second Great Awakening* in the anti-slavery movement was led in the North by religious

    A. Methodists
    B. Calvinists
    C. Anabaptists
    D. Quakers

33. Which of the following Confederate generals was from the western region of the United States?

    A. Robert E. Lee
    B. Nathan Bedford Forrest
    C. Stonewall Jackson
    D. James Longstreet

34. Albert Sidney Johnston, commander of the western Confederate forces, decided to attack General Grant's troops at Shiloh in 1862 in order to

    A. drive Union forces out of Tennessee with one swift surprise offensive
    B. regain the initiative before Grant's troops could be reinforced
    C. stall for time until his forces could be reinforced by General Beauregard
    D. stall for time while other Confederate troops destroyed bridges over the Tennessee River

35. Though sometimes used interchangeably, the terms *Copperheads* and *Peace Democrats* can be differentiated in the following way:

    A. Copperheads tended to support Lincoln's suspension of the writ of *habeas corpus*
    B. Copperheads were generally more opposed to emancipation
    C. Peace Democrats openly encouraged desertions from the Union army
    D. Peace Democrats were generally less supportive of the fugitive slave law

36. The Confederacy's war effort was financed primarily through each of the following EXCEPT

    A. taxation
    B. treasury notes
    C. tariffs
    D. loans

37. The opposition factions that surfaced within the Confederate government that hindered its effectiveness in the last half of the war was fueled by each of the following developments EXCEPT

    A. the suspension of the writ of *habeas corpus*
    B. the impressment of supplies
    C. the lack of movement against the corrupt profiteering trade
    D. conscription

38. A significant difference between the organization of Union and Confederate armies was that the Union

    A. government supplied the horses for its cavalry and artillery
    B. army had a greater complement of officers trained at military academies
    C. army used brigadier generals in its command structure
    D. army relied heavily on volunteer regiments

39. Which of the following military campaigns is generally considered to have been the MOST successful of the war?

    A. Lee's Shenandoah Valley campaign
    B. McClellan's peninsula campaign
    C. The Confederate invasion of Kentucky
    D. Grant's Vicksburg campaign

40. The *black codes* adopted by Southern governments after the war were generally harshest in South Carolina and

    A. Mississippi   B. North Carolina
    C. Kentucky   D. Georgia

41. In August of 1862, President Lincoln met with several black leaders in the White House and spoke with them of his ideas concerning the post-war situation among freed slaves. The position he advocated most strongly during this meeting was the

    A. migration of all freed slaves to Northern states
    B. separate colonization of freed slaves
    C. integration of freed slaves into white society, but with segregated institutions
    D. forced integration of freed slaves into white society and institutions

42. At the outset of the war, the Confederacy's most important advantage stemmed from its

    A. manpower   B. superior intelligence
    C. morale   D. defensive posture

43. Why did reconstruction's *carpetbag* Republican regimes begin to lose support in the North during the 1870s?

    A. Disillusionment with corrupt and mismanaged radical regimes
    B. Renewal of pro-slavery sentiment
    C. Disillusionment with the Grant administration
    D. Growing sympathy for the conquered South

44. The most frequently offered explanation for the failure of Union General George Mcclellan's peninsular campaign of 1862 is that

    A. he hesitated too long before launching his offensive
    B. he was strategically outsmarted by the Confederate commanders, Generals Lee and Jackson
    C. he was forced to withdraw troops for the defense of Washington
    D. his forces were outnumbered

45. Which of the following Confederate generals was replaced by Joseph Johnston after the battles of Chattanooga in 1862?

    A. Pierre Gustav T. Beauregard
    B. John C. Breckinridge
    C. Simon Buckner
    D. Braxton Bragg

46. Which of the following events most clearly sparked the birth and rise of the Republican party?
The

 A. Compromise of 1850
 B. Kansas-Nebraska Act
 C. Fugitive Slave Law
 D. Harper's Ferry massacre

47. In what year did the Confederacy unify command of its military forces under Robert E. Lee?

 A. 1861   B. 1862   C. 1864   D. 1865

48. The Union forces increased by a little over 500,000 during the summer of 1862, due largely to the

 A. imposition of state quotas by the federal government
 B. recruitment of volunteers
 C. loyalty of Southern Unionists
 D. implementation of a national conscription act

49. In what year did the North adopt the Enrollment Act as its federal conscription law?

 A. 1861   B. 1862   C. 1863   D. 1864

50. Which of the following events in 1861 served as an official Union reaffirmation that it had no purpose, directly or indirectly, to interfere with slavery in the states where it existed?

 A. President Lincoln's pledge of continued enforcement of the fugitive slave law
 B. The Wilmot Proviso
 C. The Walker Tariff
 D. The Crittenden-Johnson resolution

KEY (CORRECT ANSWERS)

1.	B	11.	C	21.	B	31.	A	41.	B
2.	B	12.	A	22.	D	32.	B	42.	D
3.	B	13.	B	23.	D	33.	B	43.	A
4.	A	14.	B	24.	B	34.	B	44.	A
5.	B	15.	B	25.	C	35.	B	45.	D
6.	C	16.	A	26.	C	36.	C	46.	B
7.	D	17.	A	27.	D	37.	C	47.	D
8.	D	18.	C	28.	C	38.	A	48.	A
9.	C	19.	D	29.	B	39.	D	49.	C
10.	A	20.	B	30.	B	40.	A	50.	D

TEST 2

DIRECTIONS: Each question or incomplete statement is followed by several suggested answers or completions. Select the one that BEST answers the question or completes the statement. *PRINT THE LETTER OF THE CORRECT ANSWER IN THE SPACE AT THE RIGHT.*

1. The event which most clearly brought about President Lincoln's decision to issue the Emancipation Proclamation was   1.___

    A. the Confederate invasion of Kentucky
    B. the Battle of Antietam
    C. pressure from Northern Democrats prior to the 1862 elections
    D. the Crittenden-Johnson resolution

2. Which of the following Union generals led troops at the battle of Chancellorsville?   2.___

    A. Ulysses S. Grant
    B. George McClellan
    C. Joseph Hooker
    D. George Gordon Meade

3. The battle of the Monitor against the Virginia (Merrimack), the first naval battle between ironclad ships, was significant in terms of the Civil War because it marked   3.___

    A. a major swing in the momentum of the naval war
    B. the turning of Confederate sentiment away from war
    C. the beginning of an all-out naval assault against Union ports
    D. the end of any Confederate salt-water challenges to the Union navy

4. No matter what their motives, Confederate opponents of Jefferson Davis's leadership throughout the latter half of the war most often expressed their dissent in terms of   4.___

    A. morality
    B. economics
    C. military necessity
    D. states' rights

5. In 1860, a Confederate act was passed to continue in force all the laws of the United States, so far as they were not inconsistent with the Confederate constitution. Which of the following states voted AGAINST this legislation?   5.___

    A. Georgia
    B. South Carolina
    C. Mississippi
    D. Virginia

6. The purpose of the Dix-Hill cartel of 1862 was to   6.___

    A. effect the release of all prisoners of war and address the problem of a unilateral excess of prisoners
    B. reach an agreement on the military seizure of private property
    C. reach an agreement on the treatment of black prisoners of war
    D. discuss a bilateral solution to the problem of profiteering

7. During the first half of the 19th century, the most fundamental reason for the South's failure to keep pace with modernization in the rest of the country was   7.___

    A. a low literacy rate
    B. the expense of perpetuating the slave trade
    C. protectionist tariffs
    D. the lack of diversity in its economy

8. Which of the following best describes the federal law established by the Fifteenth Amendment to the Constitution, passed by Congress in 1869? The

    A. prohibition of states to deny citizens the right to vote on grounds of race, color, or previous condition of servitude
    B. affirmation that all male citizens aged twenty-one years or older had the right to vote
    C. prohibition of racial discrimination in providing suffrage and the prohibition of literacy, property, or nativity qualifications for suffrage
    D. prohibition of states to deny citizens the right to vote on grounds of race, color, previous condition of servitude, creed, or gender

9. Approximately what percentage of the total Confederate population was comprised by slaves?

    A. 10   B. 20   C. 40   D. 50

10. Black suffrage suffered a setback in 1865, when the issue was defeated in referendums held in several Northern states. Which of the following states did not hold a referendum on the issue in 1865?

    A. Wisconsin
    B. Ohio
    C. Connecticut
    D. Minnesota

11. In the beginning years of the Civil War, officers in volunteer companies were selected by means of

    A. appointment by a state governor
    B. appointment by a regimental officer
    C. election by soldiers of the company
    D. achievement on written qualification examinations

12. Immediately following the war, all Republicans – radical, moderate, and conservative – generally agreed that

    A. Southern representatives should not be admitted to Congress
    B. Southern states should be restored to the Union as quickly as possible
    C. freedmen should participate as much as possible in the reconstruction of the states
    D. freedmen should be granted immediate suffrage

13. In which of the following states were slaves freed by state legislation, rather than by implementation of the Emancipation Proclamation?

    A. Tennessee   B. Texas   C. Kentucky   D. Arkansas

14. Although many white Union soldiers initially resisted the policy of arming blacks for the war, most of them eventually embraced it because,

    A. they found the abolitionist rhetoric of Republican radicals to be persuasive
    B. it increased the probability of commissions for white officers
    C. they could become increasingly rich as *bounty brokers*
    D. it was the only way to turn the tide of the war to the Union's favor

15. Prior to its establishment at Richmond, the Confederate capital was in the city of   15.___

    A. Charlotte   B. Montgomery
    C. Atlanta   D. Columbia

16. During the 1864 election campaign, Republican politicians and sympathizers were able   16.___
    to damage the prospects of the Democratic party by means of

    A. focusing on the war record of the Democratic candidate, George McClellan
    B. implicating Democrats in treasonous Copperhead conspiracy
    C. publicizing the high rate of military desertion in Midwestern states
    D. publicizing the pro-slavery sentiments of many Democrats

17. When the Freedmen's Bureau was finally established in 1865, it was placed under the   17.___
    authority of the _____ Department.

    A. Interior   B. War   C. Justice   D. Treasury

18. Which of the following was the most decisive issue that led to James K. Polk's nomina-   18.___
    tion as Democratic presidential candidate for the 1844 election?

    A. The annexation of Texas
    B. The negotiation of an Oregon territory
    C. The status of the New Mexico territory
    D. California statehood

19. Prior to its transfer to the War Department after the Emancipation Proclamation in 1862,   19.___
    which Union cabinet department was responsible for internal security?

    A. Interior   B. Treasury   C. State   D. Justice

20. In 1864, after the North developed a unified command system (under General Grant) to   20.___
    coordinate strategy on all fronts, which of the following was NOT a component of the
    original strategic plan devised by this command? General

    A. Benjamin Butler would move troops up the James River to threaten Richmond
    B. Meade was to lead the Army of the Potomac in attacking General Lee's Army of
       Virginia
    C. Sherman would lead a march through Georgia to cut off the Confederate troops
       from resources
    D. Sigel was to move up the Shenandoah Valley to prevent aid from reaching Lee's
       army

21. The first state to secede from the Union, in 1860, was   21.___

    A. Virginia   B. South Carolina
    C. Tennessee   D. Georgia

22. The Thirteenth Amendment changed the substance of Constitutional amendments by   22.___
    establishing a precedent for

    A. limiting the claims of the citizenry upon certain types of personal property
    B. limiting the power of the federal government
    C. defining the terms of permissible revolutionary or anti-government activities
    D. restricting state powers or expanding those of the national government

23. During the first years of the war, Union abolitionists proposed the legitimate freeing of slaves, in spite of the constitutional guarantee, by means of

    A. a simple declaration of the illegitimacy of slavery
    B. confiscating slaves as enemy property that was being used in direct aid of the rebellion
    C. enlisting as many slaves as possible in the Union armies
    D. a constitutional amendment

24. Which of the following Confederate generals led the unsuccessful campaign against Union forces at Nashville in 1864?

    A. William J. Hardee
    B. Jeb Stuart
    C. John B. Hood
    D. Joseph E. Johnston

25. The 1862 battle in which the combined casualty rate (33% of Union troops lost; 31% of Confederate troops) was the highest of the war was fought at

    A. Gettysburg
    B. Chancellorsville
    C. Vicksburg
    D. Stone's River

26. The Wade-Davis Bill of 1864 was a source of extreme political friction between the President and the legislature. This friction centered on the issue of

    A. capricious use of the Presidential veto
    B. popular sovereignty
    C. punishment of revolutionaries
    D. the President's selective application of legislation that had been approved by Congress

27. Which of the following was NOT a characteristic of the antebellum United States?

    A. Expanded education and mass communications
    B. A marked decrease in agricultural products
    C. Rapid increases in industrial output per capita
    D. A value system that emphasized change over tradition

28. Which commodity, according to most estimates, was responsible for the greatest amount of revenue during the corrupt profiteering practices of the war?

    A. Cotton   B. Steel   C. Whiskey   D. Wheat

29. The 1861-1862 Union campaign into Kentucky, which resulted in the capture of Forts Henry and Donelson, was commanded by Generals

    A. Halleck and Buell
    B. Buell and Grant
    C. Sherman and Grant
    D. McClellan and Sherman

30. The passage of the Enrollment Act, the Union's federal conscription law, sparked major antidraft and antiblack rioting in the city of

    A. Cincinnati
    B. New York
    C. Philadelphia
    D. Washington

31. As the Fort Sumter crisis intensified in 1861, Secretary of State William Seward recommended to President Lincoln that the situation might be defused by

    A. leaving soldiers stationed at Fort Moultrie where they were, without increasing the staffing at Fort Sumter
    B. allowing states the right to self-determination on the issue of slavery
    C. engaging in a foreign war over violations of the Monroe Doctrine
    D. abandoning Fort Sumter to the Confederacy

32. In what city did the Republicans hold their 1864 convention?

    A. Baltimore   B. Cincinnati
    C. Chicago   D. New York

33. Which of the following was a result of the Compromise of 1877?

    A. The rapid mobilization of Southern state militias
    B. A run-off vote in the presidential election
    C. Suffrage for all adult black males
    D. The collapse of all remaining reconstruction governments in the South

34. The bloodiest single day of the war, in which nearly 5,000 soldiers died on both sides, occurred during the battle of

    A. Vicksburg   B. Gettysburg
    C. Shiloh   D. Antietam

35. President Johnson's 1865 proclamations concerning reconstruction proposed each of the following EXCEPT

    A. restitution of all property except slaves to those taking an oath of allegiance to the Union
    B. naming a provisional governor in North Carolina
    C. recognition of Lincoln-sponsored governments in Louisiana, Arkansas, and Tennessee
    D. provision of a universal plan for the education of freedmen

36. Approximately what portion of the entire Confederate fighting force was made up of soldiers enlisted through conscription?
    One-

    A. eighth   B. fifth   C. third   D. half

37. In the South, which of the following was a gradual effect of the end of the African slave trade (1808)?

    A. The expansion of slave labor into more skilled trades
    B. A reduction in the rate of slave population increase
    C. A greater effort to keep slave families together
    D. An improvement in the physical treatment of slaves

38. In composing the Reconstruction Act of 1867, radical and moderate Republicans generally agreed upon the issue of

   A. confiscation and redistribution of land to freedmen
   B. nullification of existing Southern governments
   C. long-term disenfranchisement of ex-Confederates
   D. federally-supported schools for Southern blacks

38.____

39. The region of the Union considered to be the *mother of Republican radicalism* throughout the war and reconstruction years was

   A. the Great Lakes region
   B. New England
   C. the rural Pennsylvania-Ohio River and canal regions
   D. the border states

39.____

40. The Confederate decision in 1865 to arm slaves for battle resulted in

   A. the recruitment of black troops, but none actually serving in battle
   B. the formation and mobilization of a few small black regiments, but with no serious casualties
   C. an internal attempt to overthrow the Confederate government
   D. the death of several dozen black Confederate soldiers

40.____

41. As black troops were increasingly introduced into the Union army, President Lincoln originally planned to use them only for rear area duties, garrisoning forts, and protecting supply dumps. Which of the following was NOT a reason for this?

   A. Remaining skepticism about the suitability of black soldiers for combat
   B. The belief that black soldiers were less likely to become sick during garrison duty than white soldiers
   C. The lack of Northern resources to equip the additional forces for combat
   D. Rear-area duties would reduce the possibility of capture

41.____

42. The first Congressional Republican attack on slavery in 1862 was

   A. the creation of schools for black children in Washington
   B. an article of war prohibiting army officers from returning fugitive slaves to their masters
   C. the prohibition of slavery in all territories
   D. the abolition of slavery in the District of Columbia

42.____

43. From the period of 1860-1870, it is estimated that the material wealth of the South decreased by about _____ percent.

   A. 15   B. 25   C. 40   D. 60

43.____

44. Which of the following was not an element of the Compromise of 1850? The

   A. admission of California as a state
   B. banning of slavery in the New Mexico and Utah territories
   C. abolition of the slave trade in the District of Columbia
   D. adjustment of Texas's borders

44.____

45. Confederate soldiers and Georgia militiamen burned and destroyed large parts of the land and resources in 1864 in order to

    A. starve Sherman's troops on their way to Savannah
    B. keep Confederate property from falling into Union hands
    C. exact revenge from Southern slaves and sharecroppers in Georgia
    D. drive slaves out of the path of Sherman's march

46. Throughout the war, the European country which demonstrated the strongest pro-Southern sentiment was

    A. Spain   B. Britain   C. Portugal   D. France

47. The last state to ratify the Fifteenth Amendment was

    A. Texas
    B. Georgia
    C. Tennessee
    D. South Carolina

48. Throughout the war, armies on both sides preferred to organize entirely new regiments instead of channeling new recruits into old regiments to keep up to strength. Which of the following were reasons for this?
    I. High casualties tended to eventually replace entire regiments anyway.
    II. New regiments provided state governors with a means of patronage.
    III. The primary basis for forming regiments would have been weakened by intermingling troops from different areas and groups.
    IV. New regiments provided ambitious men a means of advancement.
    The CORRECT answer is:

    A. I, III
    B. II, IV
    C. II, III, IV
    D. I, III, IV

49. By the war's end, approximately _____ of the 3.5 million Confederate slaves had been freed directly by Northern invasion.

    A. 15,000
    B. 450,000
    C. 1.5 million
    D. 2.5 million

50. At the height of reconstruction in the 1870's, approximately what percentage of all Southern officeholders were black?

    A. 1-3   B. 15-20   C. 35-50   D. 60-70

KEY (CORRECT ANSWERS)

1. B	11. C	21. B	31. C	41. C
2. C	12. A	22. D	32. A	42. B
3. D	13. A	23. B	33. D	43. D
4. D	14. B	24. C	34. D	44. B
5. B	15. B	25. D	35. D	45. A
6. A	16. B	26. D	36. C	46. D
7. D	17. B	27. B	37. D	47. B
8. A	18. A	28. C	38. B	48. C
9. C	19. C	29. B	39. B	49. C
10. B	20. C	30. B	40. A	50. B

TEST 3

DIRECTIONS: Each question or incomplete statement is followed by several suggested answers or completions. Select the one that BEST answers the question or completes the statement. *PRINT THE LETTER OF THE CORRECT ANSWER IN THE SPACE AT THE RIGHT.*

1. Which religious group played the most significant role in the 18th-century beginnings of the antislavery movement in America? 1.___

    A. Shakers B. Mormons C. Quakers D. Catholics

2. General William T. Sherman's famous march came to an end in 1865 in the city of 2.___

    A. Columbia
    C. Savannah
    B. Wilmington
    D. Raleigh

3. The North's assurances of a quick victory in 1862 were initially cut short by 3.___

    A. Stonewall Jackson's Shenandoah Valley campaign
    B. General McClellan's failure to capture Richmond
    C. the second battle of Manassas
    D. the battle of Shiloh

4. The military successes of the 1864 Union campaign into Virginia were slowed when 4.___

    A. General Lee led a brilliant counteroffensive that temporarily divided the Union armies
    B. General Lee ordered his troops into defensive positions in trenches
    C. General Sheridan's cavalry moved in from the rear to join the fight
    D. a shocking number of Union troops were killed at Cold Harbor

5. Which of the following departments was NOT included in the Confederate cabinet? 5.___

    A. War B. Interior C. State D. Justice

6. During the Union's military campaign of 1864, General Philip Sheridan's responsibility was to 6.___

    A. reduce and devastate the Shenandoah Valley
    B. command the Army of the Potomac
    C. engage Confederate troops east of Richmond
    D. delay Johnston's troops in northwestern Georgia

7. The Union navy's chief task throughout the Civil War was 7.___

    A. to use inland waterways to transport troops deep into the Confederacy
    B. the blockade of Southern ports
    C. the defense of Northern ports
    D. to seize Southern ports

8. The *scalawags* of Southern reconstruction were drawn largely from each of the following regions EXCEPT 8.___

    A. western North Carolina and Virginia
    B. upland counties of eastern Tennessee
    C. eastern Texas
    D. northern Georgia, Alabama, and Arkansas

9. In 1862, the battle of Fredericksburg brought to head a political crisis within the Lincoln administration that centered on the

   A. conduct of Secretary of the Treasury Salmon P. Chase in securing financing for the war effort
   B. power of the executive over legislative due process
   C. influence of Secretary of State Seward on questions concerning slavery and military appointments
   D. polity of imposing the Emancipation Proclamation on an already rebellious Confederacy

10. Which of the following Southern cities offered great strategic importance by forming the junction of the Confederacy's two east-west railroads, as well as the gateway to the war industries of Georgia?

    A. Chattanooga
    B. Nashville
    C. Murfreesboro
    D. Vicksburg

11. Which of the following was NOT thought to be either an immediate or eventual consequence of the first battle of Manassas (Bull Run) in 1861?

    A. Northern optimism concerning its artillery troops
    B. A sense of inferiority among Northern officers
    C. Southern overconfidence on the home front
    D. Strengthened Northern determination

12. The Union general who led the drive through central Tennessee in 1862 was

    A. William T. Sherman
    B. William S. Rosecrans
    C. Ambrose Burnside
    D. Joseph Hooker

13. Each of the following was a factor in the weakening of the Whig party in the South during the 1840s and 1850s EXCEPT the

    A. defections to nativist parties in 1854-1855
    B. failure to pass an effective fugitive slave law
    C. increasing perception of Democrats as stronger Southern rights advocates
    D. memory of Whig President Zachary Taylor's admission of California and New Mexico as states

14. In general, the ratio of Civil War soldiers who died of disease to those killed in battle was about

    A. 1:2   B. 1:1   C. 2:1   D. 5:1

15. It is generally true that the policies of European governments toward the Civil War were determined ultimately by

    A. considerations of power and self-interest
    B. questions of ideology concerning government and sovereignty
    C. public opinion
    D. stances on the issue of slavery

16. The absence of political parties in the Confederate government system ultimately served to

    A. create a more unified front against the Union cause
    B. alienate most of the Southern aristocracy
    C. encourage corruption through its lack of consequence
    D. produce an opposition that was unmanageable

17. Which of the following Confederate cities was captured by Union Admiral David Farragut in 1862?

    A. Vicksburg
    B. Charleston
    C. New Orleans
    D. Mobile

18. The Republican party was founded in 1854 having its main issue the prohibition of

    A. slavery throughout the United States
    B. slavery in newly acquired territories
    C. slavery in the District of Columbia
    D. the slave trade throughout the United States

19. Which of the following military leaders was NOT involved in the 1862 battle at Stone's River?

    A. William T. Sherman
    B. George Thomas
    C. John C. Breckinridge
    D. Braxton Bragg

20. The Democratic Convention of 1864 affected the Republican Party by

    A. weakening Republican standing by creating a united Democratic front
    B. weakening Republican opposition by creating a Copperhead splinter in the Democratic Party
    C. helping splinter the Republican Party into feuding factions
    D. helping to consolidate Republican factions against political opposition

21. In 1865, which of the following states was represented in both the Confederate and Union cabinets?

    A. Kentucky
    B. West Virginia
    C. Tennessee
    D. Missouri

22. When William T. Sherman negotiated surrender with Joseph Johnston in 1865, each of the following was a condition proposed by Sherman EXCEPT the

    A. recognition of Southern state governments when their officials had taken an oath of allegiance
    B. guarantee of Southerners to political rights and franchises
    C. allowance of disbanded Confederate troops to deposit their arms in state arsenals
    D. immediate freedom of all slaves

23. The most significant way in which slavery inhibited the advance of modernization in the South was

    A. its extreme limitation of the upward mobility of slaves in the labor force
    B. the expense of purchasing and maintaining slaves
    C. its degradation of the status of labor among the general working population
    D. its perpetuation of the Southern reliance on agriculture

24. In 1864, Confederate general Jeb Stuart was killed by General

    A. Sheridan's cavalry raid at Yellow Tavern
    B. Meade's troops at Spotsylvania
    C. Sigel's troops in the Shenandoah
    D. Butler's troops on the James River

25. In the spring of 1862, Confederate General Thomas J. "Stonewall" Jackson died of pneumonia, which had set in after he was wounded at the battle of

    A. Fredericksburg   B. Chattanooga
    C. Chancellorsville   D. Gettysburg

26. The last major Confederate port to be sealed off by Union troops was

    A. Charleston   B. Wilmington
    C. Port Royal   D. Mobile

27. Which state was won by Stephen Douglas during the 1860 presidential election?

    A. Missouri   B. South Carolina
    C. Florida   D. Ohio

28. Which of the following most strongly supported Democratic candidate George McClellan in the presidential election of 1864?
    I. Protestant denominational groups
    II. Rural areas in which the foreign element dominated
    III. The immigrant proletariat
    IV. Skilled urban workers and professional classes
    The CORRECT answer is:

    A. I, II   B. II, III   C. I, IV   D. IV *only*

29. It is generally believed today that President Johnson's liberal granting of pardons to Southerners immediately following the war was most evidently a result of his

    A. desire to create an atmosphere of goodwill and reconciliation
    B. latent pro-slavery sentiments
    C. susceptibility to flattery and a growing bitterness toward Republicans
    D. hope for providing a Southern political counterweight to corrupt carpetbag regimes

30. Upon his election to the presidency, each of the following qualities displayed by President Lincoln tended to create an unfavorable impression EXCEPT his

    A. preoccupation with office-seekers at the expense of weightier matters
    B. social awkwardness
    C. inability to take a strong political stand on the question of union
    D. caution in making decisions

31. At the outset of the war, the Confederacy's biggest military weakness was in the area of

    A. the overall training and readiness of officers
    B. naval power
    C. morale
    D. cavalry

32. General McClellan was ultimately removed from command of the Army of the Potomac because of his

    A. Democratic politics
    B. inability to inspire his troops
    C. inability to carry out successful military operations
    D. vocal pro-slavery stance

33. Throughout the war, the rate of death from disease of black Union troops was approximately _____ that of Northern white soldiers.

    A. one-half
    B. the same
    C. twice
    D. four times

34. The main reason behind Britain's negotiation of a treaty of recognition and commerce with the Republic of Texas in the 1840s was to

    A. foster a British-Texan slave trade
    B. promote emancipation through British influence
    C. provoke a civil conflict that would weaken the United States
    D. prevent its annexation as a slave state

35. Despite President Johnson's impeachment in 1868, the President was ultimately acquitted for the reason that

    A. he used powers that were clearly discretionary
    B. he was found not to have violated the spirit of the Tenure of Office Act
    C. he managed to build a strong following among Democrats and conservative Republicans
    D. moderate congressmen did not want to weaken the institution of the executive

36. The first Confederate state capital to fall to the North was

    A. Little Rock
    B. Frankfort
    C. Columbia
    D. Nashville

37. President Lincoln's solution to the Fort Sumter crisis was to

    A. arm the fort heavily in anticipation of a Union offensive into Confederate territory
    B. send the troops at the fort only food and supplies through unarmed transports, in order to test Confederate aggression
    C. abandon the fort in the hope of preserving the Union
    D. do nothing and wait for the Confederacy to attack

38. Which of the following Confederate generals nearly captured Washington in 1864?

    A. Jeb Stuart
    B. Jubal Early
    C. James Longstreet
    D. Robert E. Lee

39. The behavior of the Confederate Vice President, Alexander H. Stephens, throughout the war can best be described as demonstrating

   A. a constant overemphasis on military matters
   B. continued attempts to undermine the Confederate executive
   C. thinly veiled sympathy for the cause of union
   D. unqualified support for the administration

40. The first Confederate invasion of the North occurred with the battle of

   A. Gettysburg
   B. Perryville
   C. Antietam
   D. Corinth

41. Which of the following was NOT an element of the original conscription law, the Enrollment Act, passed by the Union?

   A. The allowance of substitution
   B. Various occupational exemptions
   C. The permission of a drafted man to pay a commutation fee rather than serve
   D. The stimulation of volunteering through the offering of bounties

42. Which 1846 proposal advocated the banning of slavery from any territories that might be annexed as a result of the Mexican War?
   The

   A. Missouri Compromise
   B. Kansas-Nebraska Act
   C. Wilmot Proviso
   D. Walker Tariff

43. As the issue of black suffrage was discussed during the early years of reconstruction, President Johnson voiced an unwillingness to include former black Union soldiers in the electorate. What was his reason for this?

   A. Their inclusion would have doubled the size of the black electorate.
   B. Black soldiers were the most humiliating symbol of Southern defeat.
   C. Their inclusion would threaten the security of reconstruction governments.
   D. Black soldiers were generally better educated than other blacks.

44. The event or situation that most clearly turned Southerners against the cause of the Confederacy was

   A. mistreatment of Union prisoners of war
   B. the operation of the conscription act
   C. the burden of Confederate wartime taxation
   D. slavery

45. Approximately what percentage of Union soldiers deserted during the war?

   A. 2   B. 10   C. 15   D. 20

46. The main port of entry for runners of the Union blockade was the city of

   A. Port Royal
   B. Norfolk
   C. Wilmington
   D. Charleston

47. Which of the following best describes an effect of the battle at Cold Harbor in 1864?

    A. Intensification of the peace movement and the opposition to Lincoln in the North
    B. The alteration of General Lee's strategy to entrenched defense rather than mobilized offensives
    C. Heightened criticism of Jefferson Davis from high-level Confederate officials
    D. The decimation of the Union cavalry

48. The National Union movement, formed in 1866 to form a conservative (pro-Johnson) coalition in the United States government, ultimately failed because of several essential weaknesses. Which of the following was not one of these weaknesses?

    A. The increasing stridency of Andrew Johnson himself
    B. Domination of the movement by Democrats
    C. The universal popularity of radical Republicans
    D. The movement's exaggerated claim that Southerners were more obedient to the Constitution than Northerners

49. In the spring of 1862, General McClellan altered the Union strategy by planning an elaborate flanking maneuver with the Army of the Potomac against the Confederates at Centreville. His plan resulted in one of the first major disagreements to arise between McClellan and President Lincoln.
    The issue at the center of this disagreement was

    A. the overall numerical strength of Confederate forces
    B. the needless loss of life among Union soldiers
    C. the alleged superiority of the Confederate cavalry
    D. whether the objective of the Union forces should be to overwhelm the Confederate forces or to capture Richmond

50. Jefferson Davis's first secretary of state was

    A. R.M.T. Hunter
    B. John C. Breckinridge
    C. Robert Toombs
    D. Leroy P. Walker

KEY (CORRECT ANSWERS)

1. C	11. A	21. A	31. B	41. B
2. B	12. B	22. D	32. C	42. C
3. B	13. B	23. C	33. C	43. B
4. B	14. C	24. A	34. B	44. B
5. B	15. A	25. C	35. D	45. B
6. A	16. D	26. B	36. D	46. C
7. B	17. C	27. A	37. B	47. A
8. C	18. B	28. B	38. B	48. C
9. C	19. A	29. C	39. B	49. D
10. A	20. D	30. C	40. C	50. C

TEST 4

DIRECTIONS: Each question or incomplete statement is followed by several suggested answers or completions. Select the one that BEST answers the question or completes the statement. *PRINT THE LETTER OF THE CORRECT ANSWER IN THE SPACE AT THE RIGHT.*

1. In 1864, General Ulysses S. Grant ordered that no more exchanges of Confederate prisoners of war would occur until certain conditions were met. Which of the following was/were the conditions of Grant's suspension?
   The
   - I. end of Southern blockade-running
   - II. end of Confederate discrimination against black prisoners
   - III. end to the illicit profiteering trade
   - IV. release of enough Union prisoners to offset the Confederates paroled after Vicksburg

   The CORRECT answer is:

   A. I only   B. I, III   C. II, IV   D. III, IV

   1._____

2. Which of the following battles in the western theater was considered to have been a tactical victory for the Confederates?

   A. Vicksburg   B. Corinth
   C. Chickamauga   D. Chattanooga

   2._____

3. From 1862-1864, Indiana Governor Oliver P. Morton ran the state without a legislature for the reason that

   A. all appropriations were being directed to the war effort
   B. Republicans had deserted the state senate in order to deny a Copperhead-dominated legislature
   C. Peace Democrats and Copperheads had boycotted all senate sessions in order to withdraw support from the war effort
   D. the 1862 elections had been suspended by the war

   3._____

4. Just prior to the war, approximately what percentage of United States industrial capacity was possessed by the North?

   A. 35   B. 60   C. 75   D. 90

   4._____

5. Of the following Southern states, which was the first to pass through reconstruction into *home rule,* or restored state sovereignty?

   A. North Carolina   B. Tennessee
   C. Georgia   D. Arkansas

   5._____

6. The most significant effect of the development of the canal system during the mid-19th century in America was

   A. the decreasing importance of rail transport
   B. the reduction in Northern reliance on Southern agriculture
   C. an overall reduction in imports
   D. the reorientation of trade patterns along east-west lines in the North

   6._____

23

7. During the 1865 Hampton Roads peace conference between Abraham Lincoln and Alexander Stephens, each of the following was a term of surrender proposed by President Lincoln EXCEPT

   A. immediate reunion
   B. no compensation to Southerners for freed slaves
   C. no receding on the issue of emancipation
   D. an absolute end to hostilities and the disbanding of all forces

8. Which of the following was NOT among the principal killer diseases of the Civil War?

   A. Typhoid   B. Malaria   C. Dysentery   D. Influenza

9. Each of the following describes a policy held by President Lincoln at the outset of the Civil War EXCEPT

   A. opposition to the arming of blacks
   B. limited war
   C. gradual, compensated emancipation
   D. reconstruction of the Union

10. The 1864 event that most clearly strengthened support for President Lincoln's policies in the North was

    A. Sherman's march
    B. the Confederate loss of Jeb Stuart
    C. the fall of Atlanta
    D. the battle at Cold Harbor

11. The principal agency through which Northern women aided the war effort was the

    A. Young Women's Christian Association
    B. United States Sanitary Commission
    C. American Red Cross
    D. American Public Health Association

12. Each of the following was an element of President Lincoln's 1863 plan for reconstruction EXCEPT

    A. a full pardon to individuals involved in the war
    B. acceptance of the degree of emancipation already accomplished
    C. the confiscation of all private property used in direct or indirect aid of the war effort
    D. the political restoration of a state dependent upon an oath of allegiance from at least 10 percent of the voting population

13. Of the following political parties in the antebellum United States, which was NOT an abolitionist party?

    A. Free Soil   B. Republican
    C. Know-Nothing   D. Liberty

14. President Andrew Johnson's idea of reconstruction for the South included   14.____

    A. universal black suffrage
    B. the temporary designation of rebellious states to the status of territories
    C. reconstruction as primarily a legislative function
    D. the states' retention of all constitutional rights

15. It is generally believed that the Union attacks at the battle of Antietam failed because   15.____

    A. they were delivered serially instead of simultaneously
    B. superior Confederate intelligence was able to locate and isolate the component forces
    C. the Union forces were outnumbered
    D. the Confederate forces could hold fast to a defensive position

16. During the Union's 1864 military campaigns in Virginia, the ratio of Union casualties to Confederate casualties was approximately   16.____

    A. 1:3   B. 1:2   C. 1:1   D. 2:1

17. In 1863, a dramatic upsurge in pro-Union opinion occurred in Britain, largely as a result of   17.____

    A. the battle of Antietam
    B. the Emancipation Proclamation
    C. the Confederate invasion of Kentucky
    D. Lincoln's suspension of the writ of *habeas corpus*

18. An immediate consequence of the war following the final surrender of the Confederacy was the   18.____

    A. trial and execution of several Confederates for treason
    B. continued buildup of state militias in both Northern and Southern states
    C. rapid demobilization of the Union armies
    D. election of a series of *military* United States Presidents

19. Which of the following were problems associated with the Confederate conscription law that was first passed in 1862?   19.____

    I. Overall resistance to what was perceived as an encroachment on states' rights
    II. Numerous exemption categories which favored the rich
    III. The tacit encouragement of violent impressment
    IV. A provision allowing one to escape military service by hiring a substitute

    The CORRECT answer is:

    A. I, III   B. II, IV
    C. I, II, IV   D. II, III, IV

20. Approximately what percentage of Southern capital was invested in manufacturing at the outset of the war?   20.____

    A. 3   B. 15   C. 50   D. 75

21. In general, it can be said that President Lincoln's idea of reconstruction for the South was based on the idea that the main task of reconstruction was to

    A. restore control of the states to loyal citizens
    B. maintain Northern political control over the new Southern governments
    C. completely destroy the South's capacity for war
    D. free all remaining slaves from servitude

22. Throughout the war, the Confederacy failed to achieve even diplomatic recognition by a single foreign government. The most important single factor in this failure was

    A. the skill with which Union diplomats persuaded European governments away from the Confederate cause
    B. generalized European opposition to the institution of slavery
    C. fear of the consequences of war with the North
    D. the inability of the Confederacy to win enough consecutive victories to convince observers of the possibility of sustained independence

23. Throughout the war, the period of the worst morale in the North is generally considered to have been the

    A. summer of 1861   B. fall of 1862
    C. winter of 1863   D. summer of 1864

24. Each of the following was an element of the Confederate constitution EXCEPT

    A. the subordination of individual states to one central Confederate government
    B. the guarantee of slavery in all territories and states
    C. executive line-item veto power in appropriations bills
    D. the prohibition of protective tariffs

25. Of all the Confederate territory covered by William T. Sherman's troops during 1864, the greatest amount of damage was inflicted upon

    A. Georgia   B. South Carolina
    C. North Carolina   D. Virginia

26. Which of the following Union generals took over command of the Army of the Potomac from George McClellan in 1862?

    A. William T. Sherman   B. Ambrose E. Burnside
    C. Henry Halleck   D. Ulysses S. Grant

27. The purpose of the 1854 Kansas-Nebraska Act was to

    A. ban slavery in the territories of Kansas and Nebraska
    B. refer the issue of slavery in Kansas and Nebraska to popular sovereignty
    C. enact fugitive slave laws in both Kansas and Nebraska
    D. repeal the Missouri Compromise's ban on slavery in the northern Louisiana Purchase territories

28. In the entire Union military campaign from the Wilderness to Cold Harbor in 1864, approximately how many Union soldiers were lost?

    A. 12,000   B. 30,000   C. 55,000   D. 72,000

29. The Confederate Impressment Act of 1863 ultimately resulted in the

   A. reduced role of speculators in commodity markets
   B. intensification of shortages and inflation through increased resistance on the part of farmers and merchants
   C. increasing desertion of Confederate soldiers
   D. alleviation of shortages and inflation through the arbitration of a fair price for goods

30. Which of the following states did NOT call a convention to discuss the issue of secession?

   A. Kentucky   B. Arkansas   C. Virginia   D. Missouri

31. In 1865, President Johnson and the Republicans argued over the issue of black suffrage. President Johnson claimed that interfering in a state's voting qualifications was unconstitutional. Republicans responded that

   A. until a constitutional amendment could be adopted, they were in agreement
   B. the Constitution implied federal regulation of voting qualifications and standards
   C. it was no more unconstitutional than appointing provisional governors or abolishing slavery, which the executive had already done
   D. black suffrage was a moral issue, not a constitutional one

32. The reason for President Lincoln's extreme distress after the battle of Gettysburg was that

   A. Union forces continued to pursue Confederate forces across the Potomac
   B. the weakened Confederate army was not captured and destroyed after the battle
   C. Union generals continued to publicly criticize the President's leadership
   D. an appalling loss of life was suffered on both sides

33. The most decisive battle of Grant's 1862 Vicksburg campaign was fought at

   A. Jackson   B. Champion's Hill
   C. Big Black River   D. Vicksburg

34. In the spring of 1862, the Midwestern Copperhead politician Clement L. Vallandigham spoke out strongly in support of a platform that included each of the following EXCEPT the

   A. unconstitutionality of conscription
   B. repudiation of the Emancipation Proclamation
   C. deportation of free blacks to the South
   D. declaration of an armistice with the South and the restoration of the Union

35. Militarily, the Confederacy enjoyed its greatest early superiority in its

   A. infantry   B. artillery
   C. cavalry   D. volunteer pool

36. During the conferences of the Confederate cabinet and generals in the spring of 1862, Robert E. Lee pushed for the concentration of Confederate forces in the Virginia theater. Each of the following was a reason given for this plan EXCEPT

    A. enabling the army to resupply itself from the Pennsylvania countryside
    B. possibly accomplishing the capture of Washington
    C. relieving the threat to Richmond
    D. accepting that the war in the West was probably lost

36.___

37. Which of the following countries was the first to abolish slavery?

    A. France
    B. Britain
    C. United States
    D. Denmark

37.___

38. The most common reason given for the Union loss at the battle of Chancellorsville in 1862 was that

    A. Confederate General Lee did not divide his army during the engagement
    B. the Confederates outnumbered the Union forces
    C. the Union troops attempted to travel over waterways
    D. the full force of the Union Army was never engaged at one time

38.___

39. The most frequent source of friction between the Confederate government and Southern state officials regarding the issue of states' rights was probably

    A. taxation
    B. the slave trade
    C. the fugitive slave law
    D. conscription

39.___

40. Confederate General Joseph E. Johnston was relieved of command in 1864 by Jefferson Davis, ostensibly for each of the following reasons EXCEPT

    A. he failed to come to the aid of Vicksburg's besieged defenders in 1861
    B. his troops retreated to Richmond before being rescued by General Lee in 1862
    C. he failed to fight his way out of Bull Run in the first battle of Manassas in 1861
    D. he retreated from Sherman's armies all the way to Atlanta in 1864

40.___

41. Among volunteer regiments in both Union and Confederate armies, the principal basis for recruitment was most often

    A. geography   B. class   C. ethnicity   D. training

41.___

42. The election crisis of 1866 was caused by conflicting reports of results in each of the following states EXCEPT

    A. Florida
    B. Georgia
    C. South Carolina
    D. Louisiana

42.___

43. Each of the following is now considered to have been a condition that contributed to the deplorable disease-ridden condition of the Confederate prison camp at Andersonville, Georgia EXCEPT

    A. the extreme cruelty of Confederate guards
    B. the inability of Confederate officers to deal with the immense number of prisoners
    C. the poverty of the Confederacy in material resources
    D. Confederate difficulties in obtaining supplies and equipment

43.___

44. Which of the following states was NOT won by George McClellan in the presidential campaign of 1864?

    A. Kentucky
    B. Delaware
    C. Ohio
    D. New Jersey

45. Which of the following events most decisively led to the Compromise of 1850? The

    A. implementation of Oregon's territorial status
    B. annexation of Texas
    C. implementation of New Mexico's territorial status
    D. admission of California as a state

46. According to General William T. Sherman, the purpose of his armies' march to Savannah was primarily to

    A. destroy the civilian population's willingness to support the Confederate war effort
    B. capture a key Confederate port
    C. destroy the agricultural resources of the South
    D. capture a staging ground for his movement into South Carolina

47. By the end of the war, approximately what percentage of Union troops were black?

    A. 15   B. 25   C. 40   D. 60

48. Each of the following is generally considered to have been a reason for the generalized ineffectiveness of the Confederate Congress throughout the war EXCEPT

    A. a long tradition of obstructionism in legislature
    B. a tendency toward long sessions of rhetoric and oration
    C. the tendency of most powerful Confederate leaders to join the military
    D. flaws in the checks and balances provisions of the Confederate constitution

49. Of all the litigation that has occurred in the United States as a result of the Fourteenth Amendment, most of it has concerned Section

    A. 1, which defined all native-born persons as citizens and provided for equal protection of all citizens under the law
    B. 2, which provided for the proportional reduction of congressional representation in any state that withheld suffrage from a portion of its adult male citizens
    C. 3, which disqualified Confederate officials from holding office in the restored Union
    D. 4, which repudiated the Confederate debt

50. During the first year or two of the war, Confederate officers were generally of higher quality than Union officers, because

    A. the South benefited from a large number of graduates from military academies
    B. Confederate officers were often trained by foreign officers
    C. officers in the South were generally from the upper class and, therefore, more literate
    D. they earned their position solely on the basis of performance in battle

KEY (CORRECT ANSWERS)

1. C	11. B	21. A	31. C	41. A
2. C	12. C	22. D	32. B	42. B
3. B	13. C	23. D	33. B	43. A
4. D	14. D	24. A	34. C	44. C
5. B	15. A	25. B	35. C	45. D
6. D	16. D	26. B	36. D	46. A
7. B	17. B	27. D	37. B	47. C
8. D	18. C	28. C	38. D	48. D
9. D	19. C	29. B	39. D	49. A
10. C	20. B	30. A	40. C	50. A

EXAMINATION SECTION
TEST 1

DIRECTIONS: Each question or incomplete statement is followed by several suggested answers or completions. Select the one that BEST answers the question or completes the statement. *PRINT THE LETTER OF THE CORRECT ANSWER IN THE SPACE AT THE RIGHT.*

1. As a result of the Missouri Compromise, 1.____

    A. Missouri was admitted to the Union as a free state
    B. slavery was prohibited in all of the Louisiana Territory
    C. Maine was admitted to the Union as a free state
    D. all of the Louisiana Territory was open to slavery

2. William Lloyd Garrison based his opposition to slavery on the belief that it was 2.____

    A. economically unsound
    B. unconstitutional
    C. communistic in nature
    D. morally wrong

3. In 1831, a slave uprising in Virginia was led by 3.____

    A. John Brown
    B. Joseph Coxey
    C. Nat Turner
    D. Daniel Shays

4. The Liberty Party was formed by people who favored 4.____

    A. women's suffrage
    B. temperance in drinking
    C. the abolition of slavery
    D. restrictions on immigration

5. A new interest in western expansion developed in the early 1800's out of 5.____

    A. a world-wide depression originating in western Europe
    B. overcrowded conditions in the East
    C. the need of southern planters to find land open to slavery
    D. a desire to spread Christianity to the Indians

6. The loudest protests against the annexation of Texas came from the 6.____

    A. expansionists
    B. Southern planters
    C. abolitionists
    D. New England industrialists

7. Mexico broke diplomatic relations with the United States in 1845 as a protest against 7.____

    A. American settlement of New Mexico
    B. the annexation of Texas
    C. the presence of the United States Navy off the California coast
    D. the stationing of American troops south of the Rio Grande River

8. The American drive on Mexico City in 1847 was led by General 8.____

    A. Zachary Taylor
    B. Stephen W. Kearny
    C. J.D. Sloat
    D. Winfield Scott

9. The FIRST of the territories ceded by Mexico after the Mexican War to gain a large enough population to request statehood was

   A. California
   B. New Mexico
   C. Arizona
   D. Nevada

10. The Free Soil Party

    A. made no stand on the issue of slavery
    B. was composed mainly of slave owners
    C. called for the abolition of slavery
    D. opposed the extension of slavery into the territories

11. According to the principle of popular sovereignty,

    A. the Missouri Compromise line was to be extended to the Pacific Ocean
    B. slavery was to be prohibited in all of the territory gained from Mexico
    C. the people who lived in each territory were to decide whether or not slavery was to be permitted there
    D. slavery and involuntary servitude were to be abolished wherever they existed

12. The important provisions of the Compromise of 1850 came fron a series of measures presented to the Senate by

    A. William H. Seward
    B. John C. Calhoun
    C. Henry Clay
    D. Jefferson Davis

13. The Kansas-Nebraska Bill was pushed through both houses of Congress under the masterful leadership of

    A. Stephen A. Douglas
    B. Daniel Webster
    C. Salmon P. Chase
    D. Millard Filmore

14. The Republican Party was formed in

    A. 1854   B. 1856   C. 1858   D. 1860

15. The MOST dramatic change in American agriculture began in 1793 with the invention of the

    A. McCormick reaper
    B. cotton gin
    C. mowing machine
    D. combine

16. The incident which finally caused the southern states to secede from the Union was

    A. the passage of the Kansas-Nebraska Bill
    B. John Brown's raid of Harper's Ferry
    C. the election of Abraham Lincoln
    D. the Dred Scott decision

17. The Constitution of the Confederate States of America

    A. legalized the foreign slave trade
    B. provided for a protective tariff
    C. was completely different from the Constitution of the United States
    D. openly accepted the doctrine of state sovereignty

18. Four of the eight border states remained loyal to the Union during the Civil War: Delaware, Maryland, Kentucky, and

    A. Arkansas
    B. Tennessee
    C. Missouri
    D. North Carolina

19. The secession of Virginia in 1861

    A. was responsible for the Confederate attack on Fort Sumter
    B. left the Union without a good harbor
    C. deprived the Union of the services of Robert E. Lee
    D. brought France into the war on the side of the Confederacy

20. The Union campaign in the East during the Civil War centered around efforts to

    A. divide the Confederacy in two sections
    B. seize the Confederate capital at Richmond, Virginia
    C. open the Mississippi River to northern commerce
    D. capture the important southern railroad centers in South Carolina

21. All of the Civil War was fought below the Mason-Dixon line with the *important* exception of the Battle of

    A. Gettysburg
    B. Manassas
    C. Vicksburg
    D. Antietam

22. An *important* advantage which the South had in the early part of the Civil War was

    A. superior industrial resources
    B. more manpower
    C. more able military leaders
    D. a better navy and merchant marine

23. The MAJOR shortcomings of General George B. McClellan, who was, for a time, commander of the Union forces in the East, was that he

    A. had no previous experience
    B. was over-cautious
    C. lacked organizational skill
    D. was not popular with his men

24. A naval expedition under David Farragut paved the way for the Union capture in 1862 of

    A. Shiloh
    B. Richmond
    C. New Orleans
    D. Chattanooga

25. The Confederate invasion of Maryland in September, 1862, was checked by the defeat of the southern forces at

    A. Vicksburg
    B. Fredericksburg
    C. Chancellorsville
    D. Antietam

26. After March 1864, the commander of the Union armies was

    A. A.E. Burnside
    B. Ulysses S. Grant
    C. Joseph Hooker
    D. George G. Meade

27. The Union blockade of southern ports

    A. was very ineffective
    B. proved to be one of the most effective forces in overpowering the South
    C. had to be discontinued after 1862 because of a lack of Union ships
    D. was solely responsible for Lee's surrender at Appomatox

28. The battle of the Merrimac and the Monitor proved the

    A. superiority of the Union navy
    B. superiority of ironclad ships
    C. inefficiency of ironclad ships
    D. superiority of the Southern navy

29. The *Trent* incident of 1861 strained relations between the North and

    A. France
    B. Spain
    C. Great Britain
    D. Mexico

30. Great Britain and France

    A. favored the North through all of the Civil War
    B. became allies of the South early in the Civil War
    C. did not formally recognize the Confederacy
    D. provided the ships which the Union used in the blockade of southern ports

31. The Emancipation Proclamation

    A. offered a complete and final solution to the problem of slavery
    B. paved the way for a change in the Constitution that would legally abolish slavery
    C. applied to all states below the Mason-Dixon line
    D. was announced by Abraham Lincoln in his second inaugural address

32. The Copperheads were

    A. Republicans who favored the renomination of Abraham Lincoln in 1864
    B. Northerners who went south following the Civil War
    C. members of the Union Party
    D. extreme Democrats who called the Civil War a failure and urged immediate efforts to end it

33. Abraham Lincoln based his plan for southern reconstruction on his

    A. pardoning power
    B. veto power
    C. position as commander-in-chief of the armed forces
    D. power to appoint government officials

34. Andrew Johnson's plan for southern reconstruction was

    A. almost as generous as the Lincoln plan
    B. entirely different from the Lincoln plan
    C. very similar to the Congressional plan
    D. approved by Congress in 1865

35. The publisher of THE LIBERATOR, a newspaper which worked for the abolition of slavery, was

    A. Samuel G. Howe
    B. Henry Ward Beecher
    C. William Lloyd Garrison
    D. Harriet Beecher Stowe

36. Texas was NOT annexed by the United States until nearly ten years after she won her independence because

    A. most Texans wanted to remain an independent republic
    B. many Americans violently objected to admitting Texas into the Union
    C. President James Polk opposed annexation
    D. there was no legal way by which Texas could be annexed

37. The war with Mexico began when Mexican forces crossed the Rio Grande River and attacked a detachment of Americans led by

    A. Zachary Taylor
    B. Robert E. Lee
    C. Andrew Jackson
    D. William Henry Harrison

38. According to the terms of the Missouri Compromise,

    A. slavery was to be allowed in all of the Louisiana Territory
    B. Missouri was admitted to the Union as a slave state
    C. slavery was illegal in all of the Louisiana Territory
    D. Missouri was admitted to the Union as a free state

39. The idea that the United States government should keep its hands off all matters over which it had NOT been given definite authority by the Constitution became the basis for what is known as the doctrine of

    A. states' rights
    B. mercantilism
    C. squatter sovereignty
    D. federalism

40. In 1846, a provision that slavery should NEVER exist in any lands gained from Mexico was presented to Congress by

    A. John C. Calhoun
    B. David Wilmot
    C. Daniel Webster
    D. Robert Hayne

41. California was admitted to the Union as a free state under the terms of the

    A. Compromise of 1850
    B. Kansas-Nebraska Bill
    C. Missouri Compromise
    D. Great Compromise

42. Northern opinion *against* slavery was inflamed by UNCLE TOM'S CABIN, which was written by

    A. William Lloyd Garrison
    B. Harriet Beecher Stowe
    C. James Waldo Emerson
    D. Dorothea Dix

43. The people of the territories were allowed to decide whether or not they wanted to have slavery by the

    A. Dred Scott Decision
    B. Kansas-Nebraska Act
    C. Compromise of 1820
    D. Wilmot Proviso

44. In 1858, Abraham Lincoln engaged in a series of debates about slavery with

    A. Daniel Webster
    B. Stephen A. Douglas
    C. James Buchanan
    D. John C. Fremont

45. In 1859, John Brown led a group of men in an attack against the United States Armory at

    A. Sutter's Mill
    B. Fort Sumter
    C. Harper's Ferry
    D. Fort McHenry

46. The President of the Confederate States of America was

    A. John C. Breckinridge
    B. Robert E. Lee
    C. William Seward
    D. Jefferson Davis

47. Among the slave states that did NOT leave the Union at the beginning of the Civil War was

    A. Virginia   B. Arkansas   C. Tennessee   D. Missouri

48. The strategy of the South in the Civil War consisted largely of

    A. dividing the North into two separate sections
    B. capturing Washington, D.C. and other key northern cities
    C. holding out until the people of the North grew tired of the War
    D. blockading all northern ports

49. The North gained control of the Mississippi River in 1863 with the capture of Port Hudson and

    A. Vicksburg
    B. Chattanooga
    C. Shiloh
    D. Richmond

50. The naval battle between the ironclad ships Merrimac and Monitor ended

    A. in a draw
    B. when the Union Monitor was sunk
    C. when both ships were severely damaged
    D. with the destruction of the Confederate Merrimac

KEY (CORRECT ANSWERS)

1. C	11. C	21. A	31. B	41. A
2. D	12. C	22. C	32. D	42. B
3. C	13. A	23. B	33. A	43. C
4. C	14. A	24. C	34. A	44. B
5. C	15. B	25. D	35. C	45. C
6. C	16. C	26. B	36. B	46. D
7. B	17. D	27. B	37. A	47. D
8. D	18. C	28. B	38. B	48. C
9. A	19. C	29. C	39. A	49. A
10. D	20. B	30. C	40. B	50. A

TEST 2

DIRECTIONS: Each question or incomplete statement is followed by several suggested answers or completions. Select the one that BEST answers the question or completes the statement. *PRINT THE LETTER OF THE CORRECT ANSWER IN THE SPACE AT THE RIGHT.*

1. In the spring of 1862, an attempt to capture the Confederate capital at Richmond was made by Union forces led by

    A. George B. McClellan
    B. *Stonewall* Jackson
    C. Ulysses S. Grant
    D. William T. Sherman

2. The Civil War ended in

    A. 1863   B. 1864   C. 1865   D. 1866

3. Abraham Lincoln was assassinated by

    A. John Wilkes Booth
    B. Aaron Burr
    C. Alexander Stephens
    D. William H. Seward

4. The Vice President who became President upon the death of Abraham Lincoln was

    A. Andrew Johnson
    B. Ulysses S. Grant
    C. James Buchanan
    D. Zachary Taylor

5. The Missouri Compromise of 1820

    A. prohibited slavery in all of the Louisiana Territory
    B. permitted settlers in a territory to decide the issue of slavery
    C. brought a permanent end to sectional self-consciousness between the North and the South
    D. maintained the balance between slave states and free states

6. In order to keep producing large quantities of cotton, southern planters

    A. employed scientific methods
    B. gradually gave up slave labor
    C. kept looking for new lands
    D. reduced the size of most plantations

7. The progress of industry in America was *greatly* aided by the increased use of

    A. slave labor
    B. home manufacturing
    C. government controls
    D. steam power

8. The American or *Know-Nothing* Party of the mid-1800's was a semi-secret political organization opposed to

    A. big business
    B. immigrants
    C. westward expansion
    D. woman suffrage

9. In MOST cases, slaves in the South received fairly good treatment because   9.____

   A. there were strict laws against mistreating them
   B. they were ALWAYS willing and energetic workers
   C. the federal government outlined strict rules for slave owners
   D. they were valuable property and represented a heavy investment

10. Northern abolitionists helped runaway slaves to escape by using the   10.____

    A. Fugitive Slave Law   B. *liberty express*
    C. *underground railroad*   D. American System

11. Early in the 1800's, a new interest in westward expansion grew out of   11.____

    A. the needs of southern cotton growers
    B. a demand for more and better beef cattle
    C. a shortage of wheat on the world market
    D. a severe depression in the industrial Northeast

12. The war for the independence of Texas broke out as a result of   12.____

    A. the invasion of Mexico by Spanish forces
    B. severe restrictions placed on the Texans by the Mexican government
    C. the activities of an American force commanded by Zachary Taylor
    D. an attempt by France to establish a dictatorship in Mexico

13. The war for Texan independence was decided by the defeat of Mexican forces at the battle of   13.____

    A. San Jacinto   B. the Alamo
    C. Goliad   D. San Antonio

14. The Presidential election of 1844 was won by the Democratic candidate who *strongly* favored annexation and expansion: 14.____

    A. Martin Van Buren   B. John Tyler
    C. Zachary Taylor   D. James Polk

15. The Mexican War ended with the signing of the Treaty of   15.____

    A. Ghent   B. Monterrey
    C. Guadalupe-Hidalgo   D. Paris

16. The Wilmot Proviso was   16.____

    A. generally condemned in the North
    B. defeated by the Senate each time a vote was taken
    C. popular in the slave states
    D. passed by Congress over the veto of the President

17. The author of noninterference with slavery in the territories was   17.____

    A. Stephen A. Douglas   B. Abraham Lincoln
    C. John C. Calhoun   D. John C. Fremont

18. The Kansas-Nebraska Bill was

    A. favored by southern congressmen
    B. vigorously attacked in the South
    C. popular with anti-slavery forces
    D. part of the Missouri Compromise

19. The Supreme Court decision in the case of Dred Scott was written by Chief Justice

    A. Roger Taney   B. John Marshall
    C. Daniel Webster   D. John Jay

20. In effect, the Dred Scott decision meant that

    A. Congress had no power to regulate slavery in the territories
    B. the Kansas-Nebraska Act was unconstitutional
    C. slaves were no longer considered the property of their owners
    D. the Missouri Compromise was the best means of stopping the spread of slavery

21. In his inaugural address, Abraham Lincoln denied any intention of

    A. trying to enforce Union laws in the South
    B. collecting federal duties and taxes in the South
    C. interfering with slavery in the states where it legally existed
    D. allowing a Civil War to occur

22. The term *border states* refers to the states that

    A. lay between the North and the cotton states
    B. formed the southern boundary of the Confederacy
    C. lay between the United States and the frontier
    D. were affected by the Union blockade

23. The FIRST of the southern states to secede from the Union was

    A. Georgia   B. South Carolina
    C. Texas   D. Kentucky

24. The credit for the success of the Union campaign in the West belongs to

    A. *Stonewall* Jackson   B. George B. McClellan
    C. Joseph E. Johnston   D. Ulysses S. Grant

25. During the years 1861-63, the Union forces in the East

    A. had little success
    B. succeeded in capturing Richmond
    C. did not allow any invasions of Union territory
    D. defeated Confederate forces at Manassas Junction and Bull Run

26. The terms of surrender which General Grant offered to General Lee at Appomattox were

    A. very harsh
    B. turned down by the Confederacy
    C. very generous
    D. later approved by Congress

27. The need to break the Union blockade led the Confederacy to experiment with

    A. ocean-going steamboats
    B. packet ships
    C. clipper ships
    D. ironclad ships

28. Perhaps the MOST surprising part of the Civil War was that the

    A. Union was able to enforce the blockade
    B. Confederacy was able to hold out until 1865
    C. Confederacy collapsed as soon as it did
    D. South was able to negotiate treaties with England and France

29. The CHIEF method used by the South to finance the Civil War was

    A. paper money
    B. an income tax
    C. foreign loans
    D. the sale of war bonds

30. *Fourscore and seven years ago* are the opening words of

    A. the Gettysburg Address
    B. Lincoln's Second Inaugural Address
    C. the Emancipation Proclamation
    D. the Constitution of the Confederate States of America

31. Slavery in the United States was prohibited by the

    A. Emancipation Proclamation
    B. Thirteenth Amendment
    C. Fourteenth Amendment
    D. Fifteenth Amendment

32. The MOST outspoken of the Democrats who opposed the re-election of Abraham Lincoln in 1864 were called

    A. Carpetbaggers
    B. Scalawags
    C. Muckrackers
    D. Copperheads

33. Under the pressure of war needs, industry in the North

    A. increased
    B. decreased
    C. felt a severe manpower shortage
    D. suffered a severe depression

34. Abraham Lincoln's plans for southern reconstruction were

    A. adopted by Congress
    B. charitable and humane
    C. based on the *state suicide* theory
    D. carried out after his death

35. Abraham Lincoln was assassinated in April,

    A. 1863   B. 1864   C. 1865   D. 1866

36. During the Civil War, the Monroe Doctrine was challenged by the establishment of a puppet ruler in Mexico by

    A. Great Britain
    B. France
    C. Germany
    D. Spain

37. A policy of free western land was established with the passage in 1862 of the

    A. Land Ordinance
    B. Homestead Act
    C. Morrill Act
    D. Northwest Ordinance

38. Paper money without specific backing issued by the Federal government to finance the Civil War was called

    A. hard money
    B. free silver
    C. greenbacks
    D. bonds

39. Hinton R. Helper's THE IMPENDING CRISIS OF THE SOUTH attempted to prove that in the South slavery had the WORST effect on

    A. families of wealthy slave owners
    B. owners of fewer than ten slaves
    C. the middle class
    D. non-slaveholding whites

40. Which one of the following statements applies to the South during the Reconstruction Era?

    A. Control of the southern economy by the plantation aristocracy was shattered.
    B. The Democratic Party maintained control of the Senate despite Radical Republican control in the House of Representatives.
    C. The Ku Klux Klan dominated southern state legislatures.
    D. The *black codes* were enacted to protect the voting rights of Negroes.

41. Which one of the following was a BASIC reason for the passage of the Fifteenth Amendment?
    The

    A. Supreme Court's decision that the Civil Rights Act of 1866 was unconstitutional
    B. desire to assure the Negro's permanent status as a free man by replacing the Emancipation Proclamation with an amendment
    C. conviction of many Radical Republicans that penalties provided by the Fourteenth Amendment for disfranchising the Negro were inadequate
    D. general feeling throughout the nation that Negro advances warranted such a step

42. Which one of the following events MOST immediately preceded the end of the Reconstruction period in the South?
    The

    A. second inauguration of Ulysses S. Grant as President
    B. adoption of the Fourteenth Amendment
    C. election of Rutherford B. Hayes as President
    D. impeachment of Andrew Johnson

43. The demand for *resumption* in the 1870's was a demand that the United States government restore the

    A. gold standard
    B. unlimited coinage of silver
    C. issuance of greenbacks
    D. redemption of paper currency with metallic money on demand

44. The issue over which the Republican and Democratic parties differed MOST sharply in the three decades after the Civil War was

    A. tariff
    B. imperialism
    C. railroad regulation
    D. banking reform

45. In what respect was the situation of the American farmer in the 1920's different from that of the American farmer in the period 1865-1900?
    He

    A. faced foreign competition because of the expansion of agricultural production in Canada, Latin America, Australia, and Europe
    B. faced a decline in American exports of food and other farm products
    C. had inadequate credit facilities and high interest charges
    D. bought supplies and equipment in a protected market and sold his crops in a competitive world market

46. During which one of the following decades was there the LEAST resistance to Negro participation in government by the existing state governments in the South?

    A. 1855-1865
    B. 1865-1875
    C. 1900-1910
    D. 1950-1960

47. In which one of the following respects was the period between 1850 and 1860 in the United States MOST different from the period between 1840 and 1850?

    A. Emphasis on the establishment of a national banking system
    B. Concern over federal regulation of interstate commerce
    C. Recurring crises over sectional issues
    D. Desire to abandon the policy of isolation

48. During the pre-Civil War period, MOST immigrants settled in the North and West because

    A. the South discouraged them by discriminatory legislation
    B. they preferred small farms rather than the large plantation holdings of the South
    C. they could not compete with the slave labor of the South
    D. they encountered no discrimination in these regions

49. The Republican Party platform in 1860 contained a plank on slavery which advocated the

    A. abolition of slavery in all states and territories of the Union
    B. prohibition of expansion of slavery into the territories
    C. emancipation of the slaves in areas where it existed with just compensation to owners
    D. emancipation of all slaves with provision for economic assistance to the freed slaves

50. Which group was MOST likely to win the sympathy of Southerners during the middle decades of the nineteenth century?

    A. Copperheads
    B. Carpetbaggers
    C. Liberal Party
    D. Scalawags

KEY (CORRECT ANSWERS)

1. A	11. A	21. C	31. B	41. C
2. C	12. B	22. A	32. D	42. C
3. A	13. A	23. B	33. A	43. D
4. A	14. D	24. D	34. B	44. A
5. D	15. C	25. A	35. C	45. B
6. C	16. B	26. C	36. B	46. B
7. D	17. C	27. D	37. B	47. C
8. B	18. A	28. B	38. C	48. C
9. D	19. A	29. A	39. D	49. B
10. C	20. A	30. A	40. A	50. A

TEST 3

DIRECTIONS: Each question or incomplete statement is followed by several suggested answers or completions. Select the one that BEST answers the question or completes the statement. *PRINT THE LETTER OF THE CORRECT ANSWER IN THE SPACE AT THE RIGHT.*

1. The MOST popular method of travel in the United States from the east coast to the west coast during the period 1849-1869 was

    A. transcontinental railroad
    B. ship and wagon train via the isthmus of Panama
    C. ship around Cape Horn
    D. wagon train across the country

2. Though Congress had levied a tax on personal incomes during the Civil War, the Supreme Court FIRST declared such a tax unconstitutional during President Cleveland's administration because the

    A. Civil War income tax law had been upheld as a war measure
    B. Civil War income tax law was never tested in the Supreme Court before it was repealed in 1873
    C. passage of an income tax law over President Cleveland's veto made a Supreme Court test obligatory
    D. Supreme Court was ineffectual during the Civil War and the years that followed

3. Henry Clay's American system was designed to

    A. strengthen the political power of the West as against the East and South
    B. compromise differences between North and South on tariff legislation
    C. facilitate expansion to the Pacific coast
    D. reduce sectional differences by creation of a unified economy

4. The traditional method of determining the expansion of slavery into new territories by Congressional enactments that defined its limits was abandoned in the case of the

    A. Northwest Territory   B. Louisiana Territory
    C. Mexican Cession   D. Oregon Territory

5. Daniel Webster reversed his traditional stand in regard to states' rights in the

    A. Dartmouth College Case
    B. Webster-Hayne Debates
    C. debate on the Compromise of 1850
    D. Kansas-Nebraska Bill

6. The various government land acts passed prior to the Civil War had the effect of _____ the minimum of acres which had to be purchased and _____ the cost per acre.

    A. reducing; decreasing   B. increasing; increasing
    C. reducing; increasing   D. increasing; decreasing

7. In the election of 1860, Abraham Lincoln's Republican Party advocated the

   A. abolition of slavery throughout the United States
   B. abolition of slavery in the territories only
   C. prevention of the extension of slavery into the territories
   D. adoption of the principle of squatter sovereignty

8. Lincoln's Emancipation Proclamation had an important effect on Great Britain's policies toward the Confederacy because it strengthened sympathy with the North among British

   A. landowners   B. workers
   C. exporters   D. manufacturers

9. Which one of the following statements is CORRECT concerning economic conditions in the South from 1865 to 1900?

   A. By 1900, the South was manufacturing more woolen goods than New England.
   B. The proportion of the nation's manufacturing done in the South was much the same in 1900 as it was in 1860.
   C. There was a steady rise in the price of cotton from the close of the Civil War to 1900.
   D. Landlords and merchants to whom sharecroppers were indebted encouraged diversified farming.

10. In which instance was an important compromise involving the North and the South arrived at without public debate or open publication?

    A. 1820   B. 1833   C. 1850   D. 1877

11. Which statement BEST describes the major objective of the Populist movement? It

    A. was directed against monopolistic control of western lands by large-scale entrepreneurs
    B. advocated government ownership and operation of agricultural lands
    C. sought to achieve lower railroad rates through the elimination of marginal unprofitable roads
    D. was an effort by segments of our agricultural population to restore profits in the face of unfavorable market and price conditions

12. Which was the MOST important international factor that led to agrarian depressions in the U.S. from the early 1870's to the 1890's?

    A. An almost uninterrupted international price decline
    B. Japanese rise to power in the Far East
    C. European wars
    D. European emigration to America

13. All of the following factors helped bring about the annexation of Texas in 1845 EXCEPT:

    A. Texas was becoming a center of foreign intrigue
    B. Mexican officials finally recognized Texas' independence
    C. Americans were caught up in the fever of manifest destiny
    D. Annexation was an important campaign issue in the election of 1844

14. Which one of the following may NOT be included in a list of the influences of the *frontier* on American history? It

    A. acted as a possible *safety valve* for economic unrest
    B. retarded the development of the industrial East
    C. had a democratizing influence on the country
    D. was a spur at once to individual initiative and collective social action

15. Which one of the following men was MOST unlike the other three in his views regarding slavery?

    A. Wendell Phillips
    B. Henry Ward Beecher
    C. Daniel Webster
    D. John G. Whittier

16. The doctrine of popular sovereignty was FIRST stated in the

    A. Wilmot Proviso
    B. Compromise of 1850
    C. Kansas-Nebraska Act
    D. Missouri Compromise

17. Of the following, the two leading senators who made possible the passage of the Compromise of 1850 were

    A. Calhoun and Clay
    B. Clay and Webster
    C. Clay and Douglas
    D. Calhoun and Webster

18. Which one of the following was NOT a provision of the Compromise of 1850?

    A. A strict fugitive slave law
    B. Missouri to be admitted as a slave state
    C. Texas to be given ten million dollars for surrendering territory to the federal government
    D. California to be admitted as a free state

19. Which of the following did NOT represent a clash of interest between the United States and Great Britain during the Civil War?
    I. Trent Affair
    II. Monitor v. Merrimac
    III. Alabama Raids
    IV. Maximilian Affair

    The CORRECT answer is:

    A. I, IV   B. I, III   C. II, III   D. II, IV

20. Which one of the following reasons was NOT advanced by the Radical Republicans who opposed the Lincoln-Johnson plans for Reconstruction?

    A. They believed that southern leaders should be punished by being stripped of civil rights and property.
    B. They wanted to restore the balance of power between the executive and legislative branches of the government which had existed prior to the war.
    C. They feared that granting the ballot to the Negro would drive Southern whites into the Democratic Party.
    D. Southern governments set up under the Lincoln-Johnson plan were under the control of the Democratic Party.

21. Which of the following is NOT true regarding the 14th Amendment?
It

    A. provided for a proportionate reduction in representation in the House when a state denied the franchise
    B. abrogated the *three-fifths* clause, thereby increasing Southern representation in the House of Representatives
    C. was formulated because of widespread doubt as to the constitutionality of the Civil Rights Act
    D. honored the payment of both the Union and the Confederate debt

22. Which one of the following promises was NOT made to Southern Democratic leaders in return for their support in the election of Hayes over Tilden?
The

    A. withdrawal of federal troops from the South
    B. appropriation by Congress of substantial funds for internal improvements in the South
    C. downward revision of the high post-war tariffs
    D. appointment of at least one Southerner to the Cabinet

23. Which one of the following statements is NOT true concerning the currency situation after the Civil War?

    A. At the close of the war, farmers urged that government bonds be redeemable in greenbacks.
    B. In 1875, Congress provided for the redemption of greenbacks by specie.
    C. In order to maintain purchasing power, businessmen favored continuance of greenback currency.
    D. At his inauguration, President Grant favored redemption of government bonds in gold.

24. Which one of the following was NOT a factor responsible for the rapid settlement of the Far West from 1870 to 1890?

    A. Transportation facilities
    B. Increased immigration
    C. Government soil conservation policies
    D. New methods of fencing

25. Which of the following statements does NOT describe an essential factor of the Economic Revolution (1865-1900) in the U.S.?
The

    A. acquisition of a labor supply sufficiently large and cheap for the purposes of industry
    B. acquisition of colonies containing many valuable raw materials
    C. discovery and the exploitation of natural resources such as iron, coal, copper, oil
    D. growth of a domestic market and the development of foreign markets

26. Which of the following developments could be observed in education in the United States during the period from 1865-1900?
    I. Educational facilities increased faster than population.
    II. Graduate studies were offered by an increasing number of universities.
    III. There was a growing interest in adult education and in library building.
    IV. The teaching profession achieved adequate standards throughout the nation.

    The CORRECT answer is:

    A. II, III, IV
    B. I, II, III, IV
    C. I, II, III
    D. I, III, IV

27. Which one of the following was NOT advocated by the American farmer between 1870-1890 in his attempt to solve his problems?

    A. Cooperative marketing of produce
    B. Government regulation of interstate carriers
    C. Contraction of the currency to raise prices
    D. Political action through the formation of third parties

28. Which group of states created from territories acquired before the Civil War was admitted to the Union after 1900?

    A. Oklahoma, New Mexico, Arizona
    B. Minnesota, Michigan, Wisconsin
    C. Washington, Oregon, Utah
    D. Nevada, Wyoming, Idaho

29. The purpose of Henry Clay's *American System* was to

    A. prevent the dissolution of the Union over the slavery issue
    B. isolate the United States from foreign entanglements
    C. unify the sections of the country by having the federal government meet their economic needs
    D. win the South from its allegiance to John Calhoun

30. Which one of the following was NOT a provision of the Omnibus Bill of 1850?

    A. A stricter fugitive slave law was to be enacted
    B. Adjustment of the Texas-New Mexico boundary
    C. Slavery was to be prohibited in the District of Columbia
    D. California was to be admitted as a free state

31. Which one of the following was NOT part of the platform of the Republican Party in the Presidential Campaign of 1860?

    A. Support of local option with regard to the question of slavery in the territories
    B. No interference with slavery in the states
    C. Support of the protective tariff
    D. Promise of free public land to settlers

32. Which one of the following statements is NOT true of the *New South* after the Civil War?

    A. The agricultural revolution touched the South less than any other section of the country.
    B. Though farms were smaller, farm tenancy was more widespread.
    C. The most striking difference between the *New South* and the *Old South* was the rise of industry and manufacturers.
    D. Since immigration avoided the South, there was a severe shortage of cheap labor.

33. Which one of the following statements would NOT correctly apply to the West after the Civil War?

    A. The generation after the Civil War witnessed the most extensive movement of population in our history.
    B. Many new states with a taste for social and political experiments arose in the West.
    C. The region of the Great Plains was one in which Eastern farming methods could best be applied.
    D. The Plains environment necessitated a modification of social attitudes and of political and legal institutions.

34. Which of the following statements would NOT appear in a chapter in a textbook on American history entitled, *The Economic Revolution - 1865-1900?*

    A. It was the dream of Jefferson that his country was to be a great agrarian democracy.
    B. The U.S. was progressing in the direction of a diversified, self-sufficing nation, as advocated by Hamilton.
    C. Spokesmen of big business were appealing for Hamilton's interpretation of the Constitution as against Jefferson's.
    D. Within two generations of Jefferson's death, the value of American manufactured products was almost triple that of the agricultural.

35. Which of the following was NOT a reason for the general expansion of U.S. agriculture after 1860?

    A. Lack of competition in world markets from other countries
    B. Opening up of new agricultural land
    C. Growth of population
    D. Improved transportation facilities

36. Which of the following was NOT an issue on which Daniel Webster took a prominent position?
    The

    A. Compact Theory
    B. Compromise of 1850
    C. Dartmouth College Charter
    D. Yazoo land claims

37. Which one of the following pairs expressed a similar purpose or principle concerning the slavery issue?

    A. Northwest Ordinance - Compromise of 1850
    B. Missouri Compromise - Kansas-Nebraska Act

C. Dred Scott Decision - Freeport Doctrine
D. Free Soil Party - Republican Party (1854-1860)

38. Which of the following statements BEST explains England's neutrality in the American Civil War?
    I. The effect of the Emancipation Proclamation
    II. Dependence on Northern exports of wheat
    III. The democratic attitudes in the English government
    IV. The surpluses of Egyptian cotton
    V. English war profits
    The CORRECT answer is:

    A. I, II, IV
    B. III, IV, V
    C. I, IV, V
    D. I, II, V

39. The pair which does NOT represent a cause and effect relationship is

    A. Tenure of Office Act - Impeachment of Andrew Johnson
    B. National Banking Acts - Establishment of the Independent Treasury System
    C. Black codes - Civil Rights Bill
    D. Ku Klux Klan - Force Acts (1870-1871)

40. Which of the following may be CORRECTLY considered as contributing to the rapid development of the West between 1865 and 1900?
    I. Federal government's liberal land grants
    II. High prices offered for farm products
    III. Marked increase in migration from Europe
    IV. Protection of the farmers' market through tariff legislation
    The CORRECT answer is:

    A. I, III
    B. II, IV
    C. I, IV
    D. II, III

41. In connection with the slavery issue, the *gag rule* was fought on the floor of Congress in the 1830's by

    A. Henry Clay
    B. William Lloyd Garrison
    C. John Quincy Adams
    D. James G. Birney

42. On which one of the following policies were Clay and Calhoun LEAST in harmony?

    A. Declaration of war on England in 1812
    B. Tariff of 1816
    C. Chartering the Second Bank of the United States
    D. Election of John Quincy Adams

43. The two men who were MOST in agreement in the debate on the Compromise of 1850 were

    A. Clay and Calhoun
    B. Calhoun and Webster
    C. Clay and Webster
    D. Seward and Webster

44. Which of the following were considered by Southerners to be attacks on slavery?
    I. Tallmadge Amendment
    II. Wilmot Proviso
    III. Ostend Manifesto
    IV. *The Impending Crisis*

    A. II,III,IV   B. I,III,IV   C. I,II,III   D. I II,IV

45. What is the CORRECT chronological order of the following events?
    I. John Brown's raid
    II. Dred Scott decision
    III. Lincoln-Douglas debates
    IV. Founding of the Republican Party

    The CORRECT answer is:

    A. II, IV, III, I
    B. III, II, I, IV
    C. IV, III, II, I
    D. IV, II, III, I

46. Which statement is CORRECT in regard to the Kansas-Nebraska Act? It

    A. made Kansas free and Nebraska slave
    B. repealed the Missouri Compromise
    C. admitted Kansas as a slave state
    D. repealed the Compromise of 1850

47. Which of the following is TRUE of the election of 1850?

    A. Lincoln obtained a large popular majority.
    B. Republicans were a minority in each house of Congress.
    C. Douglas lost practically all the Southern popular vote to Breckinridge.
    D. Lincoln was elected by a narrow majority of electoral votes.

48. During the American Civil War, England

    A. refrained from declaring her neutrality
    B. recognized the independence of the Confederacy
    C. recognized the Confederacy as a belligerent
    D. obtained sufficient cotton from the South to keep its factories going

49. The opponent of Lincoln in the election of 1864 was

    A. Fremont   B. McClellan   C. Greeley   D. Stanton

50. A famous case in the Civil War period in which the Supreme Court held that neither the President nor Congress could declare martial law in places where civil courts were open was

    A. Mississippi vs. Johnson
    B. ex parte Milligan
    C. Georgia vs. Stanton
    D. ex parte McCardle

KEY (CORRECT ANSWERS)

1. C	11. D	21. D	31. A	41. C
2. B	12. A	22. C	32. D	42. D
3. D	13. B	23. C	33. C	43. C
4. C	14. B	24. C	34. C	44. D
5. C	15. C	25. B	35. A	45. D
6. A	16. B	26. C	36. D	46. B
7. C	17. B	27. C	37. D	47. B
8. B	18. B	28. A	38. D	48. C
9. B	19. D	29. C	39. B	49. B
10. D	20. C	30. C	40. A	50. B

TEST 4

DIRECTIONS: Each question or incomplete statement is followed by several suggested answers or completions. Select the one that BEST answers the question or completes the statement. *PRINT THE LETTER OF THE CORRECT ANSWER IN THE SPACE AT THE RIGHT.*

1. An excellent example of the Supreme Court's refusal to increase the power of the central government at the expense of state governments in the field of regulating business is

   A. Gibbons vs. Ogden, 1824
   B. Slaughter House cases, 1873
   C. Wabash vs. Illinois, 1886
   D. Pollock vs. Farmers Loan and Trust Company, 1895

2. The MOST valuable form of aid given by the Federal government to railroads in the period after the Civil War was

   A. land grants
   B. loans
   C. subsidies
   D. tariff remission on rails

3. Which one of the following may CORRECTLY be considered a result of the influence of the other three?
   The

   A. influx of large numbers of immigrants
   B. rise of big business
   C. urbanization of American life
   D. increased mechanization of agriculture

4. Which one of the following BEST states a principle established by the Dred Scott decision?

   A. Congress could abolish slavery in the territories.
   B. Congress could not legislate concerning slavery in the territories.
   C. Slaves residing in free territory automatically gained freedom.
   D. The territories, through popular sovereignty, had the sole right to decide the question of slavery within their limits.

5. Which one of the following boundary disputes was settled in a manner DIFFERENT from the others?
   _____ boundary.

   A. Maine
   B. Oregon
   C. Texan
   D. Louisiana Territory

6. Which one of the following terms has been used to characterize the social and cultural life in the United States during the period 1870-1900?
   The

   A. Tragic Era
   B. Age of Hate
   C. New Freedom
   D. Gilded Age

54

7. The 19th century American statesman who was the leading proponent of the theory of the concurrent minority, which guaranteed to large economic interests and geographic units a veto on the majority determination was

   A. John C. Calhoun
   B. Henry Clay
   C. Stephen A. Douglas
   D. Daniel Webster

7._____

8. Which one of the following permitted settlers in the Louisiana Territory to decide the question of slavery for themselves?
   The

   A. Dred Scott Decision
   B. Missouri Compromise
   C. Wilmot Proviso
   D. Kansas-Nebraska Act

8._____

9. Lincoln's Emancipation Proclamation

   A. contained a forceful indictment of slavery
   B. was based on military necessity
   C. declared all slaves in all the slave states to be free
   D. was issued after a succession of military victories by the North

9._____

10. The years immediately following the Civil War were similar to the years immediately following the War of 1812 because in both periods

    A. the executive and legislative branches were controlled by different parties
    B. the legislatures were unable to pass necessary laws
    C. the Presidents were successful military leaders but unsuccessful in civil office
    D. for practical purposes, no effective opposition groups operated in Congress

10._____

11. One of the arguments used by those who favored high tariff rates following the Civil War was that high tariffs would

    A. promote a greater volume of world trade
    B. encourage the development of new industries
    C. stop the growth of huge industrial combinations
    D. keep prices and wages low

11._____

12. The Missouri Compromise (1820), the Compromise of 1850, and the Kansas-Nebraska Act (1854)

    A. were a series of laws passed by Congress
    B. concerned the status of slavery in the Western territories
    C. dealt with sectional disputes which finally led to civil war
    D. all of the above

12._____

Questions 13-14.

DIRECTIONS: Questions 13 and 14 refer to the following chart.

13. During Period _____ on the time line above, the Civil War occurred.   13.____
    A. A   B. B   C. C   D. D

14. The Reconstruction Era *generally* refers to Period _____ on the time line above.   14.____
    A. A   B. B   C. C   D. D

15.   15.____

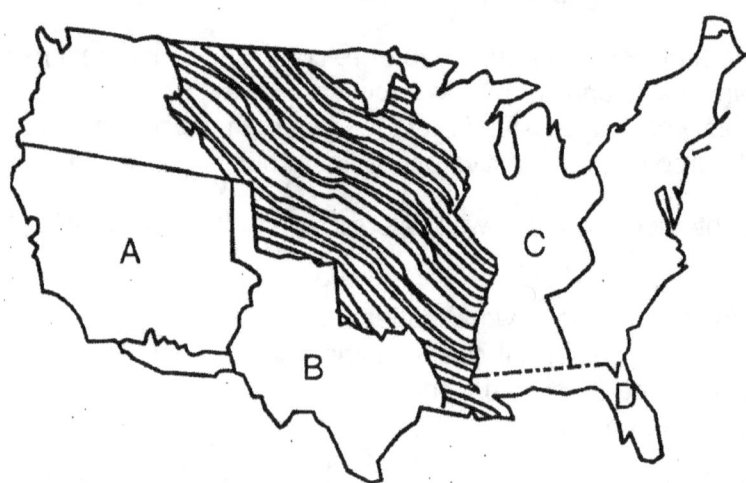

Which of the territory areas above did Mexico cede to the United States after losing the Mexican War?

    A. A   B. B   C. C   D. D

16. The invention of new farm machinery after 1850 contributed to   16.____

    A. the growth of New York as a manufacturing city
    B. the introduction of several new crops
    C. an increase in the size of farms
    D. a decline in farm production

17. The strategy of the North for winning the Civil War was to   17.____

    A. hold out until the South tired of war
    B. gain foreign aid
    C. conquer by dividing the Confederacy in two
    D. capture General Lee

18. From the end of the Civil War until 1900, the pace of industrial change in the United States

    A. grew faster and faster
    B. was unchecked by panics or depressions
    C. remained relatively slow
    D. was halted by the growth of labor unions

19. The spectacular growth of industry following the Civil War was

    A. limited almost entirely to the Northeast
    B. not evident in the Midwest
    C. not confined to any one section of the country
    D. based on a very unstable foundation

20. The FALSE statement about the Northwest Ordinance is that it

    A. was a law which told how U.S. territories should be governed
    B. told how new states would be admitted to the Union
    C. guaranteed the personal liberties of people living in the territories
    D. told how states could peacefully leave the Union

21. The Battle of Gettysburg was considered a MAJOR turning point in the

    A. Revolutionary War   B. War of 1812
    C. Civil War   D. Spanish-American War

22. Which invention had the GREATEST impact upon the political institutions of nineteenth-century America?

    A. Airplane   B. Atomic bomb
    C. Cotton gin   D. Automobile

Question 23.

DIRECTIONS: Question 23 is based on the following passage.

Convinced that the old parties had only tried to sidestep the burning issue of the day, they believed that the time had come to organize a new party. By joining with the Free-Soilers party, they were confident that they could march to victory in 1856 or certainly in 1860.

23. The *burning* issue which had been sidestepped was

    A. free and unlimited coinage of silver
    B. the extension of slavery into the territories
    C. the annexation of Oregon
    D. civil service reform

24. By _____ Congress started a great tide of westward migration.

    A. placing Indians on reservations
    B. passing the Reconstruction Acts
    C. promoting soil conservation
    D. passing the Homestead Act

25. The Missouri Compromise was dead and a new act, which would let the territories decide for themselves whether to be slave or free, would take its place. The basic principle of this new act is called

    A. states' rights
    B. direct democracy
    C. Manifest Destiny
    D. popular sovereignty

Question 26.

DIRECTIONS: Question 26 shows a newspaper headline from the first half of the nineteenth century. Decide which man's actions might have led to that headline.

26. VICE PRESIDENT CHARGES THAT NEW TARIFF BENEFITS NEW ENGLAND FACTORY OWNERS AT EXPENSE OF SOUTHERN PLANTERS AND WESTERN FARMERS

    A. Henry Clay
    B. Andrew Jackson
    C. Daniel Webster
    D. John C. Calhoun

27. America's emergence as a MAJOR industrial country occurred between

    A. the War of 1812 and the Mexican War
    B. the Mexican War and the Civil War
    C. the Civil War and World War I
    D. World War I and World War II

28. From 1860 until 1885, national politics in the United States were controlled by the _____ Party.

    A. Progressive
    B. Democrat
    C. Republican
    D. Whig

29. The gold conspiracy of 1869 was due, in part, to the over-trusting nature of President

    A. Andrew Johnson
    B. Ulysses S. Grant
    C. Rutherford B. Hayes
    D. James A. Garfield

30. In the election of 1872, Ulysses S. Grant was opposed by New York editor

    A. Horace Greeley
    B. Samuel J. Tilden
    C. Jay Gould
    D. William Lloyd Garrison

31. The disputed election of 1876 was settled by

    A. an Electoral Commission
    B. the Supreme Court
    C. the Electoral College
    D. the House of Representatives

32. In the politics of the decade after the Civil War, the issue of slavery focused on whether

    A. racial equality should be the foremost national priority
    B. slavery should be permitted to exist in the territories
    C. slavery should be eliminated where it already existed in the states
    D. the foreign slave trade should be reopened

33. Republican policies toward the South during the post-Civil War Reconstruction Era can be described MOST accurately as

    A. aiming consistently to protect the interests of postwar big business at the expense of the newly freed slaves
    B. leading to unparalleled corruption among the entrenched carpetbagger governors and their allies in the Black dominated legislatures of the defeated states
    C. leading to significant but only partially implemented constitutional changes on the state level in the South and also on the national level
    D. leading to an effective program of land redistribution that gave to large numbers of newly freed slaves *forty acres and a mule*

34. The strategy of the Confederacy at the start of the Civil War was based on all of the following assumptions EXCEPT:

    A. Cutting the North in two by seizing Washington and thrusting northward into Maryland and Pennsylvania would force the North to sue for peace
    B. The dependence of Great Britain and France on Southern cotton would lead them to grant diplomatic recognition and give military aid to the Confederacy
    C. Arming the slaves would help the South to offset superior Northern manpower
    D. Southern control of the port of New Orleans would induce the states in the upper Mississippi Valley to join the Confederacy

35. Which one of the following was NOT included in the program advocated by Henry Clay?

    A. An independent treasury
    B. A protective tariff
    C. Federal aid for internal improvements
    D. A centralized banking system

36. Which one of the following parties reflected a wave of intolerance in the United States? The

    A. Loco-focos   B. Hunkers
    C. Know-Nothings   D. Anti-Masonic Party

37. Which one of the following permitted settlers in the Louisiana Territory to decide the question of slavery for themselves? The

    A. Dred Scott Decision   B. Missouri Compromise
    C. Wilmot Proviso   D. Kansas-Nebraska Act

38. The election of Lincoln to the Presidency in 1860 was similar to that of Wilson in 1912 because in each case the

    A. Democratic candidate won
    B. election had to be decided by the House of Representatives
    C. winner benefited by a split in the opposition party
    D. winner scored a huge majority of the popular vote

39. The MAJOR purpose of the blockade during the Civil War was to prevent

    A. English volunteers from going to the South
    B. export of cotton to Europe

C. Confederate officials from going to Europe
D. the Russian fleet from visiting the South

Question 40.

DIRECTIONS: In Question 40, select the letter preceding the item that does NOT belong to the group.

40. Abolitionists

    A. John Brown
    B. William Lloyd Garrison
    C. Abraham Lincoln
    D. Harriet Beecher Stowe

41. A section of the United States in which the Democratic party had been dominant from 1860 to the 1960's was the

    A. Northeast
    B. Middle West
    C. South
    D. Far West

42. During most of the 19th century, the United States did NOT restrict immigration because

    A. the Bill of Rights forbade restrictions
    B. few Europeans wished to come here
    C. internal expansion created a demand for cheap labor
    D. the rate of population increase was slow

43. *A house divided against itself cannot stand.*
    The author of the above quotation is

    A. Robert E. Lee
    B. Daniel Webster
    C. Stephen A. Douglas
    D. Abraham Lincoln

44. In the United States, all of the following were important concerns of the humanitarians of 1820-30 EXCEPT the

    A. abolition movement
    B. treatment of the insane
    C. public school movement
    D. welfare of migrant laborers

45. All of the following were important cities in the South before the Civil War EXCEPT

    A. Atlanta
    B. Birmingham
    C. Charleston
    D. Richmond

46. The GREATEST opposition in the North to the Compromise of 1850 developed over the

    A. territorial organization of New Mexico and Utah without reference to slavery
    B. assumption of the Texan debt
    C. fugitive slave law
    D. adjustment of the Texan boundary

47. Which one of the following groups of states seceded AFTER the firing on Fort Sumter?

    A. Maryland, Kentucky, Missouri, Delaware
    B. Texas, Missouri, Virginia, Florida

C. Virginia, Tennessee, North Carolina, Arkansas
D. Louisiana, Texas, Virginia, Missouri

48. Which one of the following was NOT important as a factor in keeping England neutral during the Civil War?
The

A. sympathy of her commercial class with the Union cause
B. dependence of England on western wheat
C. anti-slavery sentiments of English liberals
D. support of the English working class for the Union cause

49. Which of the following were characteristic of the economic situation in the United States during the last half of the nineteenth century?
   I. The taking up of free land by farming families
   II. The adoption of a strong national conservation program to preserve our dwindling national resources
   III. The absence of nationwide panics and depressions
   IV. The outbreak of violent strikes, both local and general
   V. Expansion and concentration in industry

The CORRECT answer is:

A. II, III, IV
B. I, IV, V
C. I, III, V
D. II, IV, V

50. When the Missouri Compromise was adopted, which of the following statements about the United States were TRUE?
   I. The Tallmadge amendment to the bill dealing with Missouri's application for statehood had been adopted by both houses of Congress.
   II. Delaware was a slave state.
   III. The *Liberator* had been regularly published for some time.
   IV. The representation of free states in the House of Representatives exceeded the representation of the slave states in the House.

The CORRECT answer is:

A. I, II
B. II, IV
C. I, III
D. III, IV

KEY (CORRECT ANSWERS)

1. B	11. B	21. C	31. A	41. C
2. A	12. D	22. C	32. B	42. C
3. C	13. B	23. B	33. C	43. D
4. B	14. C	24. D	34. C	44. D
5. C	15. A	25. D	35. A	45. B
6. D	16. C	26. D	36. C	46. C
7. A	17. C	27. C	37. D	47. C
8. D	18. A	28. C	38. C	48. A
9. B	19. C	29. B	39. B	49. B
10. D	20. D	30. A	40. C	50. B

EXAMINATION SECTION
TEST 1

DIRECTIONS: Each question or incomplete statement is followed by several suggested answers or completions. Select the one that BEST answers the question or completes the statement. *PRINT THE LETTER OF THE CORRECT ANSWER IN THE SPACE AT THE RIGHT.*

1. Most of the iron and munitions used by the Confederacy during the war were manufactured in the state of 1._____

    A. South Carolina
    B. Alabama
    C. Virginia
    D. Tennessee

2. At the outset of the war, the main advantage of the South over the North was a 2._____

    A. defensive military posture
    B. long martial tradition
    C. superior navy
    D. larger population pool from which to draw forces

3. Which of the following Northern states was the last to emancipate its slaves? 3._____

    A. Massachusetts
    B. New York
    C. Pennsylvania
    D. New Jersey

4. Most of the *carpetbaggers* who came to the South in postwar years were 4._____

    A. privateers from New England who sought business opportunity
    B. Union army veterans who had fought in the South
    C. politicians with no base of support in the North
    D. native Southerners who were repatriating

5. The Crittenden Compromise, proposed in 1860, would have protected slavery in the _____ territory for as long as the area held territorial status. 5._____

    I. Utah
    II. New Mexico
    III. Kansas
    IV. Nebraska

    The CORRECT answer is:

    A. I, II
    B. II *only*
    C. I, III, IV
    D. III, IV

6. The South had made considerable progress toward developing its own industrial boom in the 1850s. Which of the following offers the best explanation for why it never grew to play a major role in the Southern economy? 6._____

    A. Tariffs and other barriers were repeatedly imposed by the Northern-dominated legislature.
    B. It was impossible, because of slavery, to secure foreign investment in industrial enterprise.
    C. Most Southerners did not think industry would become a significant economic factor.
    D. Most of the capital in the south was invested in slave-maintained plantations.

7. For generations after the Civil War, the stronghold of Republican sentiment throughout the Solid South was concentrated in the

    A. Mississippi Delta
    B. Gulf Coast region
    C. Southern highlands
    D. smaller benchlands

8. With his repulse at Sabine Pass in 1863, which Union general was forced to abandon his plan of an amphibious invasion of Texas?

    A. George Thomas
    B. Nathaniel P. Banks
    C. David Farragut
    D. Benjamin Butler

9. The seat of the pro-slavery puppet government that was established in *Bleeding Kansas* was located in

    A. Shawnee Mission
    B. Topeka
    C. Wyandotte
    D. Wichita

10. Which of the following was the first Indian tribe to declare an allegiance to the Confederate cause in 1861?

    A. Chickasaw   B. Miami   C. Cherokee   D. Choctaw

11. Throughout the war effort, northern blacks made several significant contributions toward assisting slaves who had been liberated from the South. The most noteworthy of these was probably

    A. the provision of medical care for freed slaves and their families
    B. the establishment of schools for children of freed slaves
    C. political lobbying for the cause of abolition
    D. the organization of freed slaves into self-sufficient urban enclaves

12. On February 4, 1861, the new provisional government of the Confederate States of America was organized in

    A. Atlanta
    B. Richmond
    C. Columbia
    D. Montgomery

13. Which of the following played the largest role in the Union's financing of its war effort?

    A. Taxation
    B. The issuance of *greenback* paper currency
    C. Bond sales
    D. Tariffs

14. At the outset of the war, the strategy that President Lincoln appeared determined to pursue was that of

    A. establishing a border around the Confederacy to assure Southerners of goodwill, and wait for Union sentiment to overtake the state governments
    B. aggressive penetration and defeat of the South
    C. entering Southern territory for the sole purpose of locating and recruiting Southern Unionists
    D. relying solely on a naval blockade to bring economic pressure to the South

15. The candidate of the Know-Nothing Party in the election of 1856 was

    A. Martin Van Buren
    B. John Fremont
    C. Millard Fillmore
    D. Abraham Lincoln

16. For both the North and the South, the most crucial border state throughout the war was

    A. Delaware
    B. West Virginia
    C. Tennessee
    D. Maryland

17. Which of the following was/were reasons for the failure of the Confederacy's attempts at *Cotton Diplomacy* with Britain during the Civil War?
    I. Decreased demand for cotton in Britain
    II. Increased British cotton imports from Egypt and India
    III. A bad grain harvest in Britain, remedied by United States grain imports
    IV. Union sales of captured cotton to Britain

    The CORRECT answer is:

    A. I *only*
    B. I, III
    C. II, III, IV
    D. I, II, III, IV

18. The *black codes* adopted by former Confederate states in 1865-1866 generally imposed restrictions on each of the following for freed slaves EXCEPT

    A. assembly
    B. ownership of land
    C. ownership of weapons
    D. travel

19. The Civil Rights Bill which eventually became the 14th Amendment to the Constitution was passed by Congress in

    A. 1864   B. 1866   C. 1870   D. 1874

20. Late in the war, which of the following was a term sometimes used as a synonym for a Confederate soldier?

    A. Butternut
    B. Grayneck
    C. Roundhead
    D. Copperhead

21. The final battle of Gen. George Gordon Meade's Overland Campaign was fought in 1864 at

    A. North Anna
    B. Cold Harbor
    C. Spotsylvania
    D. Fort Fisher

22. Union forces at the 1864 battle at Nashville were led by

    A. George Thomas
    B. John A. Logan
    C. John M. Schofield
    D. George Gordon Meade

23. The *Liberator,* an abolitionary newspaper, was first published in 1831 by

    A. Elijah Lovejoy
    B. William Lloyd Garrison
    C. Frederick Douglass
    D. John Brown

24. After Lincoln's victory in the 1860 presidential election, Southern Democrats controlled the
    I. House
    II. Senate
    III. Supreme Court

    The CORRECT answer is:

    A. I, II
    B. III only
    C. II only
    D. I, II, III, IV

25. Who was the first field commander of Union forces in the Civil War?

    A. Irvin McDowell
    B. Nathaniel Lyon
    C. Winfield Scott
    D. George McClellan

26. Which of the following generals was responsible for overseeing the reconstruction process in the state of Texas?

    A. Daniel Sickles
    B. William Sherman
    C. John Pope
    D. Philip Sheridan

27. The main reason for the relatively higher casualty rate among black Union soldiers, compared to whites, was that

    A. they were added to Union regiments late in the war without proper training
    B. they were generally ordered into more dangerous combat situations
    C. they outnumbered white soldiers in close combat
    D. Confederate officers would kill black soldiers rather than take them prisoner

28. From the beginning of his administration, Andrew Johnson suffered from a number of serious disadvantages. Which of the following was NOT one of these?

    A. Public rumors of drunkenness and misconduct
    B. Stubbornness and inflexibility
    C. A fundamental lack of integrity
    D. The nature of the political support attracted by his reconstruction plan

29. The second state to secede from the Union, on January 9, 1861, was

    A. Georgia
    B. Mississippi
    C. Louisiana
    D. Florida

30. The primary concern of most Americans immediately following the war was

    A. recovering from a post-war economic slump
    B. the problem of restoring the former Confederate states
    C. the mode of punishment for those who had rebelled
    D. the status of the institution of slavery in the South

31. The *Bloody Angle* was an area of heavy fighting in the battle at

    A. Gettysburg
    B. Antietam
    C. Spotsylvania
    D. Shiloh

32. The first important policy battery between President Lincoln and congressional Radical Republicans was fought over the readmission of _____ to the Union.   32.____

 A. Arkansas   B. South Carolina
 C. Louisiana   D. Tennessee

33. Approximately what percentage of Southern whites were slave owners in the antebellum South?   33.____

 A. 25   B. 45   C. 65   D. 85

34. The party responsible for the failure of the 1860 Crittenden Compromise was   34.____

 A. the Supreme Court
 B. the House of Representatives
 C. Abraham Lincoln
 D. the Senate

35. The Confederate Department of Alabama and West Florida, whose primary wartime responsibilities were defending Mobile and Pensacola from naval attack, was commanded by   35.____

 A. Maj. Gen. Stephen D. Lee
 B. Maj. Gen. Braxton Bragg
 C. Joseph E. Johnston
 D. Lt. Gen. Leonidas Polk

36. At the outset of 1863, the only military operations that would have a bearing upon the outcome of the war were those in   36.____

 A. Virginia and the Carolinas
 B. Virginia and Kentucky
 C. the Carolinas and Georgia
 D. Texas and Virginia

37. Each of the following was an element of the 1860 compromise advocated by Kentucky Senator John Crittenden EXCEPT   37.____

 A. the prohibition of slavery above the Missouri Compromise line
 B. compensation to owners of *rescued* slaves
 C. emancipation in the District of Columbia
 D. the self-determination of future new states regarding slavery

38. By far, the most active state in the operation of the *underground railroad* was   38.____

 A. Ohio   B. Illinois
 C. Pennsylvania   D. Iowa

39. In the antebellum South, where slaves were often given religious instruction, these teachings most often emphasized   39.____

 A. ritual   B. faith   C. doctrine   D. morality

40. Each of the following was a *political* general in the Union Army EXCEPT

    A. Daniel Sickles
    B. James Garfield
    C. Irvin McDowell
    D. Benjamin Butler

41. Which of the following cities served as the starting point for General Sherman's march to the sea?

    A. Atlanta
    B. Bowling Green
    C. Chattanooga
    D. Knoxville

42. Which of the following was NOT an element of the *Anaconda Plan* proposed by Union General-in-Chief Winfield Scott in 1861?
    A

    A. march from the Mississippi River to the Atlantic
    B. strong line of Federal positions on the Western border
    C. strong thrust down the Mississippi Valley
    D. blockade of Southern ports

43. Approximately what percentage of the Union's armed forces were composed of foreign-born men?

    A. 5
    B. 10
    C. 20
    D. 40

44. In which Southern state was Jefferson Davis captured by Union forces in April of 1865?

    A. Georgia
    B. South Carolina
    C. Florida
    D. Virginia

45. In the eyes of many observers, the 1864 Battle of Cold Harbor proved that

    A. Union troops were much more poorly trained and disciplined than their Confederate counterparts
    B. cavalry alone could not win a battle
    C. the Confederates were unwilling to negotiate any terms other than total independence
    D. the Union was willing to sacrifice a high number of casualties to ensure victory

46. Which of the following served as the Confederate secretary of the navy?

    A. George W. Randolph
    B. John C. Breckinridge
    C. Leroy Pope Walker
    D. Stephen Mallory

47. Each of the following was considered to be a stronghold of *Copperheads* in the North during the latter years of the war EXCEPT

    A. Illinois
    B. Michigan
    C. Indiana
    D. Ohio

48. Which of the following states attempted to remain neutral in the Civil War after its secession delegates refused to secede?

    A. Kentucky
    B. Missouri
    C. Maryland
    D. Delaware

49. Regarding the readmission of the Southern states to the Union, President Lincoln's belief seems to have been that

    A. the establishment of a representative government, with a proportionate number of black legislators, would be sufficient
    B. they had forfeited all their rights and must undergo the same process as any other territory for acceptance as a state
    C. it would be up to Congress to devise the conditions under which readmission would be carried out
    D. since they had never legally withdrawn, it would be a simple and informal matter

50. Among the following religious groups, which played the most important role in antebellum abolitionist leadership?

    A. Unitarians
    B. Methodists
    C. Episcopalians
    D. Roman Catholics

KEY (CORRECT ANSWERS)

1. B	11. B	21. B	31. C	41. C
2. A	12. D	22. A	32. A	42. A
3. D	13. C	23. B	33. A	43. C
4. B	14. B	24. D	34. C	44. A
5. B	15. C	25. A	35. B	45. D
6. D	16. D	26. D	36. A	46. D
7. A	17. D	27. D	37. C	47. B
8. B	18. B	28. C	38. A	48. B
9. A	19. B	29. B	39. D	49. D
10. D	20. A	30. A	40. C	50. B

TEST 2

DIRECTIONS: Each question or incomplete statement is followed by several suggested answers or completions. Select the one that BEST answers the question or completes the statement. *PRINT THE LETTER OF THE CORRECT ANSWER IN THE SPACE AT THE RIGHT.*

1. During the war, much of the outrage felt by Southerners concerning their treatment at the hands of Union forces centered on the example of General Benjamin Butler's occupation of the city of

    A. Pensacola
    B. Jackson
    C. New Orleans
    D. Mobile

2. In 1855, abolitionist John Brown and his sons traveled to _____ to make it a haven for antislavery settlers.

    A. Oregon Territory
    B. West Virginia
    C. New Mexico Territory
    D. Kansas

3. Economic growth in the North during the war was fueled by each of the following factors EXCEPT

    A. the invention and mass production of the mechanical reaper
    B. the expansion of the labor market by the addition of freed slaves
    C. protective tariffs
    D. profiteering

4. During the first forty years after the American Revolution, Southerners were often divided among themselves on political issues. Among these, the most divisive was probably

    A. civil rights
    B. international trade
    C. banking and financial policy
    D. slavery and abolitionism

5. Which of the following is generally considered to be U.S. Grant's best-fought campaign of the Civil War?

    A. Vicksburg
    B. Lookout Mountain
    C. Port Hudson
    D. Shiloh

6. From 1863 onward, which Southern state was divided into two civil government jurisdictions, one Unionist and one Confederate?

    A. Louisiana
    B. Tennessee
    C. Arkansas
    D. North Carolina

7. After the congressional elections of 1866, the first action undertaken by the Radical Republican Congress was to

    A. impose military reconstruction on the Southern states
    B. exclude the Southern votes from the electoral college
    C. refute the legitimacy of the existing state governments in the former Confederate states
    D. bar Southern representatives from the House and Senate indefinitely

8. Throughout most of the war, the primary mission of the Army of the Potomac was to

    A. inflict irreversible damage and loss upon the Army of Northern Virginia
    B. defend Washington
    C. protect Chesapeake ports from land assaults
    D. capture Richmond

9. The main reason for Lincoln's replacement of George Gordon Meade with U.S. Grant as commander of the Army of the Potomac was that

    A. Grant had powerful allies in the Lincoln cabinet
    B. Meade had not aggressively pursued General Lee's army after the victory at Gettysburg
    C. Grant's Western campaigns had been more successful than any Union campaign to date
    D. Meade had not protected his flank at Gettysburg and nearly lost the battle

10. The first important reconstruction act, passed in 1867, was largely the work of

    A. Thaddeus Stevens   B. Andrew Johnson
    C. Charles Sumner   D. John Sherman

11. The primary idea behind the Declaration of Immediate Causes, drafted by Christopher Memminger in 1860, was that

    A. blacks and whites were considered unequal under the terms of the United States Constitution
    B. Lincoln's suspension of the writ of habeas corpus was illegal
    C. the attack on Fort Sumter was an act of defense
    D. South Carolina was justified in seceding from the Union

12. In what way did the Republicans avert defeat in the election of 1864?

    A. Placing Andrew Johnson on the ticket
    B. Tabling the issue of emancipation
    C. *Supervision* of balloting in the border states
    D. Joining with War Democrats to form the Union Party

13. In both the Union and Confederate armed forces, the *buck and gag* was a

    A. means of hauling a battery and ordnance
    B. strategy for striking the flank of an opponent
    C. means of punishing enlisted men
    D. type of musket load

14. The last state to secede from the Union in June of 1861 was

    A. Texas   B. Virginia   C. Arkansas   D. Tennessee

15. Lincoln's Emancipation Proclamation formally freed slaves in
    I. specific conquered areas in the South
    II. the Confederate states still in rebellion
    III. the border states
    IV. all United States territories

    The CORRECT answer is:

    A. I, II   B. II only   C. II, III, IV   D. III, IV

16. Which of the following served as secretary of the navy in the administration of Abraham Lincoln?

    A. Gideon Welles
    B. Edward Bates
    C. David Farragut
    D. Simon Cameron

17. Which of the following statements about the American Colonization Society is true?

    A. Its chapters existed mostly in northern states.
    B. Most of its funds were directed toward establishing a colony of free blacks in Africa.
    C. It was more extreme than most abolitionist groups.
    D. It was initially dominated by northern abolitionists

18. In the mid-1800s, the statehood of _____ appears to be the event that permanently tipped the balance of sectional power to the North.

    A. Oregon   B. California   C. Colorado   D. Kansas

19. The outbreak of the Civil War sparked a renewed debate in the North about the nature of black Americans. Most of the abolitionists based their arguments for racial equality on

    A. physical and mental capacities
    B. the Christian doctrine that all were equal in the sight of God
    C. cultural differences
    D. the words of the United States Constitution

20. The most populous state of the deep South was

    A. Florida
    B. Mississippi
    C. Alabama
    D. Georgia

21. Which of the following offers the best explanation for the Republicans' selection of Andrew Johnson as Lincoln's running mate in the 1864 election? He was

    A. a former slaveowner who could attract votes from the border states
    B. an intellectual who could strike a balance to Lincoln's folksy, unread image
    C. a staunch Lincoln loyalist who would galvanize the electorate
    D. little-known and therefore inoffensive to voters

22. Which of the following was a heavy artillery piece, invented by the Confederates, that saw service both on ironclads and in seacoast fortifications?

    A. Blakely gun
    B. Dahlgren gun
    C. Brooke rifle
    D. Howitzer

23. The Confederate victory that gave General Lee the confidence to launch a second invasion of the north occurred in 1863 at

    A. Petersburg
    B. Spotsylvania
    C. Chancellorsville
    D. Antietam

24. Which of the following factors played the most significant role in bringing about the Panic of 1857?
The

   A. Missouri Compromise
   B. collapse of the shipping industry
   C. revocation of the National Bank's charter
   D. overbuilding of railroads

25. General Grant was made general-in-chief of the armed forces after the

   A. battle at Vicksburg
   B. fall of Atlanta
   C. victory at Forts Henry and Donelson
   D. conquest of Chattanooga

26. During the wave of foreign settlement that occurred in the United States in the 1840s and 1850s, which of the following states was most strongly *nativist*, or resistant to immigrant participation in civil society?

   A. Massachusetts   B. Kentucky
   C. Florida   D. Wisconsin

27. The purpose of the Edmunds Resolution of July 20, 1868 was to

   A. take control of the scheduling of congressional sessions
   B. assume partial control of the armed forces by gaining consensual powers over the army's general-in-chief
   C. give Congress, and not the states, the power to ratify constitutional amendments
   D. exclude certain Confederate states from the electoral college

28. In large part, the Confederacy's war effort was financed by a $500,000 loan from the state of

   A. South Carolina   B. Alabama
   C. Georgia   D. Mississippi

29. Which of the following can fairly be said to be a result of the extreme, violent fringe of the abolitionist movement in the North?
The

   I. endangerment of civil rights such as free speech and freedom of the press
   II. hastening of the emancipation of United States slaves by several years
   III. growth of divisive sectionalism
   IV. deferral of other reform movements

   The CORRECT answer is:

   A. I, III   B. II *only*
   C. I, III, IV   D. I, II, III, IV

30. In which of the following Northern states was slavery prohibited by the Ordinance of 1787?

   A. New Jersey   B. New York
   C. Pennsylvania   D. Ohio

31. The largest cavalry engagement of the Civil War occurred at the Battle of

   A. Brawner's Farm
   B. Franklin's Crossing
   C. Horseshoe Ridge
   D. Brandy Station

32. The results of the Emancipation Proclamation included
   I. a splintering of the Southern alliance
   II. an increase in desertion from Union forces
   III. a strengthening of the North's moral cause
   IV. increased opposition to intervention among foreign commoners
   The CORRECT answer is:

   A. I, III
   B. II, III, IV
   C. III, IV
   D. I, II, III, IV

33. The first serious bloodshed of the Civil War occurred just after the inauguration of Abraham Lincoln in riots in the streets of

   A. Pittsburgh
   B. Alexandria
   C. Baltimore
   D. Gettysburg

34. Each of the following Southern states began its reconstruction process under the Lincoln administration EXCEPT

   A. Texas
   B. Louisiana
   C. Virginia
   D. Tennessee

35. What was the means by which the Confederate states attempted to attract the sympathies of England and France during the Civil War?

   A. Offering lucrative shipbuilding contracts
   B. Seeking an endorsement of states' rights
   C. Distributing propaganda about Northern aggression
   D. Withholding cotton exports

36. Of the following Southern states, which was the last to be returned to *home rule* after the process of reconstruction?

   A. Florida   B. Alabama   C. Texas   D. Virginia

37. In March of 1865, Confederate General Joseph E. Johnston surrendered to William T. Sherman after losing the battle at _____, North Carolina.

   A. Bentonville
   B. Averasborough
   C. Fayetteville
   D. Goldsboro

38. The Congressional Committee on the Conduct of the War, an entity within the United States Congress during the Civil War, could best be described as a

   A. strong moral prosecutor of military misconduct
   B. radical think tank devoted to the cause of emancipation
   C. political tool of anti-Lincoln Republicans
   D. fiscally immoderate financer of the Union war effort

39. Which of the following amendments to the Constitution gave the United States Supreme Court the power to protect the basic civil rights of all citizens?

    A. Twelfth
    B. Thirteenth
    C. Fourteenth
    D. Fifteenth

40. Who led the failed Camden expedition in Arkansas in 1864?

    A. John M. Thayer
    B. Nathaniel P. Banks
    C. Thomas Ransom
    D. Frederick Steele

41. The most critical foreign crisis facing the United States immediately after the war had to do with a violation of the Monroe Doctrine by

    A. Canada   B. Russia   C. France   D. Britain

42. The primary purpose of Blazer's Scouts, a Union force organized by General George Crook, was to

    A. locate and destroy Quantrill and his raiders
    B. hunt down and destroy blockade runners
    C. devalue the Confederate currency through counterfeiting
    D. destroy the Partisan Rangers operating in Virginia

43. The basic premise of Congress' first reconstruction act, passed in 1867, was that

    A. the Confederacy was an enemy country to be occupied by the conquering army
    B. the former Confederate states had never lawfully seceded
    C. the former Confederate states, with their large black populations, were not practicing representative government
    D. no lawful government existed in the seceded states

44. In which of the following states in 1860 did slaves outnumber free whites?

    A. Alabama
    B. Mississippi
    C. Georgia
    D. Louisiana

45. Which of the following was granted statehood in 1861?

    A. Oregon
    B. Colorado
    C. California
    D. Kansas

46. Who led the Union Army of the Cumberland at the battle of Chickamauga in September of 1863?

    A. Gordon Granger
    B. William S. Rosecrans
    C. Henry Halleck
    D. George Armstrong Custer

47. The most significant result of the Supreme Court's 1857 Dred Scott decision was that

    A. slavery could not be barred from any United States territories
    B. black slaves could not sue in federal courts
    C. the Missouri Compromise was invalidated
    D. black slaves were not considered United States citizens

48. Shortly after the Virginia Convention approved secession, a small force of Confederate volunteers occupied the city of   48.____

    A. Alexandria
    C. Annapolis
    B. Yorktown
    D. Washington, D.C.

49. It was Senator Charles Sumner's scathing oration against the _____ that provoked his beating at the hands of Congressman Preston Brooks of South Carolina.   49.____

    A. doctrine of nullification
    B. actions of pro-slavery men in Kansas
    C. passage of the Fugitive Slave Law
    D. passage of the Kansas-Nebraska Act

50. Which of the following Confederate states approved secession by the narrowest margin?   50.____

    A. Florida   B. Missouri   C. Virginia   D. Arkansas

KEY (CORRECT ANSWERS)

1. C	11. D	21. A	31. D	41. C
2. D	12. D	22. C	32. B	42. D
3. B	13. C	23. C	33. C	43. D
4. C	14. D	24. D	34. A	44. B
5. A	15. B	25. D	35. D	45. D
6. C	16. A	26. B	36. A	46. B
7. D	17. B	27. D	37. A	47. A
8. D	18. B	28. B	38. C	48. A
9. B	19. B	29. D	39. C	49. B
10. D	20. D	30. D	40. D	50. C

TEST 3

DIRECTIONS: Each question or incomplete statement is followed by several suggested answers or completions. Select the one that BEST answers the question or completes the statement. *PRINT THE LETTER OF TEE CORRECT ANSWER IN THE SPACE AT THE RIGHT.*

1. Which of the following was an anti-slavery activist who died defending his press in Alton, Illinois in 1837?   1.____

   A. Charles Francis Adams
   B. William Wells Brown
   C. William Lloyd Garrison
   D. Elijah Lovejoy

2. In which of the following states were slaves freed by the 13th Amendment, rather than by state legislation or the Emancipation Proclamation?   2.____

   A. West Virginia
   B. Arkansas
   C. Kentucky
   D. Tennessee

3. On February 17, 1865,   3.____

   A. the Union Department of California was folded into the Department of the Pacific
   B. the city of Charleston was evacuated in anticipation of the arrival of Gen. William Sherman
   C. the first Confederate blockade runner was captured by the U.S.S. Sabine of the Union Navy
   D. Thomas *Stonewall* Jackson died of pneumonia

4. After the Battle of Antietam, President Lincoln replaced Gen. George McClellan with   4.____

   A. George Thomas
   B. Joseph Hooker
   C. Henry Halleck
   D. Ambrose E. Burnside

5. Throughout the Civil War, compared to their eastern counterparts, Union soldiers from the West were generally most different in their   5.____

   A. ratio of losses to victories
   B. questionable loyalty
   C. average age
   D. lack of discipline

6. In the 1861 Battle of Bird Creek, Confederate Colonel Douglas Cooper led about 1,400 soldiers against a group of about 1,000 pro-Union Indians composed mostly of   6.____

   A. Choctaws and Chickasaws
   B. Cherokees and Creeks
   C. Seminoles and Cherokees
   D. Creeks and Seminoles

7. The results of the 1858 Lincoln-Douglas debates included   7.____
   I. Lincoln's defeat of Douglas for the Senate seat
   II. the alienation of Southern Democrats from Douglas
   III. the rise of Lincoln to national prominence
   The CORRECT answer is:

   A. I *only*   B. I, II   C. II, III   D. III *only*

8. Which of the following states did Abraham Lincoln win in the election of 1864?

   A. New Jersey
   B. Kentucky
   C. Maryland
   D. Delaware

9. On December 20, 1860, the *Committee of Thirteen* met in

   A. Richmond to draft the new Confederate Constitution
   B. Washington to plan the offensive strategy of the Union Army
   C. Montgomery to vote on secession
   D. Washington to attempt to avert disunion

10. In what year were all Confederate war leaders granted a presidential pardon?

    A. 1866   B. 1868   C. 1870   D. 1877

11. Which of the following states was most generally opposed to the idea of secession?

    A. Maryland   B. Kentucky   C. Delaware   D. Missouri

12. The _____ probably did the most to drive the nation to Civil War.

    A. Fugitive Slave Act of 1853
    B. Kansas-Nebraska Act
    C. Compromise of 1850
    D. Wilmot Proviso

13. Ideally, a Civil War field battery consisted of _____ guns of the same caliber.

    A. 2   B. 4   C. 6   D. 8

14. Which of the following cities served as the Union point of departure for nearly all Union efforts to open the upper Mississippi or penetrate into the Southern interior?

    A. Cairo
    B. St. Louis
    C. Bowling Green
    D. Louisville

15. Which of the following was the presidential candidate of the Free Soil Party in the 1848 elections?

    A. Frederick Douglass
    B. Martin Van Buren
    C. William Lloyd Garrison
    D. John Brown

16. Which of the following Southern states was readmitted to the Union on June 25, 1868, but returned to military control after expelling blacks from its legislature?

    A. Virginia   B. Georgia   C. Arkansas   D. Texas

17. Among the reasons for the basic instability of the Confederate government, the most significant was probably

    A. the effectiveness of Union intrigue
    B. the youth and inexperience of its membership
    C. the disagreement over the location of the capital city
    D. its predication on the right to secession

18. Historians generally agree that the most important factor in the downfall of the Confederacy was the

   A. destruction of the Southern countryside
   B. Union naval blockade of Southern ports
   C. spread of popular abolitionist sentiment
   D. force of the Union armies

19. The first fighting to occur between elements of the North and South after Lincoln's inauguration took place in

   A. Texas   B. New York
   C. Florida   D. South Carolina

20. In part, the Confederacy's war effort was financed by a loan from the treasury of

   A. Germany   B. France
   C. the Netherlands   D. Great Britain

21. The battle at _____ in 1865 is generally thought to be the last battle of any importance in the Civil War.

   A. Goldsboro   B. Lynchburg
   C. Petersburg   D. Five Forks

22. The purpose of the Force Acts, passed by Congress in 1870 and 1871, was to

   A. permit military enforcement of black suffrage in the South
   B. permit military supervision of state legislatures in the South
   C. invalidate the *black codes* adopted by several states
   D. protect blacks from the violence of night-riding terrorists

23. The fourth state to leave the Union on January 11, 1861 was

   A. Alabama   B. Tennessee
   C. Kentucky   D. Georgia

24. Which of Andrew Johnson's cabinet members was secretly serving congressional radical Republicans as a spy and informer?

   A. W.W. Holden   B. Carl Schurz
   C. Edwin M. Stanton   D. Henry Stanbery

25. During the mid-1800s, the people of the South increasingly turned from a strong nationalist tendency toward sectionalism. Which of the following was NOT an important factor that helped to bring about this shift?

   A. Reaction to legislation that seemed designed to help the North while inhibiting the South
   B. A long agricultural depression that ended in 1832
   C. The perception that slavery was a doomed institution
   D. The invention of the cotton gin

26. The first Civil War engagement between Generals Grant and Lee took place at

   A. Spotsylvania   B. Manassas Junction
   C. Cold Harbor   D. Plank Road

27. The *Bread Riot* of 1863 occurred in the Confederate city of

    A. Montgomery
    B. Savannah
    C. Richmond
    D. Augusta

28. The most significant reason for Stephen Douglas's loss of the 1960 presidential election to Abraham Lincoln was that

    A. Lincoln was able to win a small measure of support in the South
    B. Lincoln carried the most populous states
    C. the new states of California and Oregon made the difference
    D. Southern Democrats had split from Douglas's party to nominate another candidate

29. The Union Army that was formed latest in the war was the Army of

    A. the Southwest
    B. the Shenandoah
    C. Kansas
    D. the Frontier

30. In the Confederate national campaign of 1863, Jefferson Davis was criticized by opponents for his policies concerning each of the following EXCEPT

    A. taxation
    B. habeas corpus
    C. property rights
    D. conscription

31. Which of the following industries did NOT experience wartime growth in the North?

    A. Agriculture
    B. Textiles
    C. Petroleum
    D. Maritime shipping

32. A Union defeat at the battle of Shiloh was prevented by the arrival, on the evening of the first day, of the army of General

    A. U.S. Grant
    B. Philip Sheridan
    C. Don Carlos Buell
    D. William T. Sherman

33. Of the following, which was the last Southern city to fall under Union control in the latter years of the war?

    A. Wilmington
    B. Richmond
    C. Montgomery
    D. Mobile

34. In 1860, the U.S. Navy Yard at Norfolk was captured by Confederate forces, largely because the Union had failed to send military reinforcements. Which of the following best explains the Union's failure to protect the installation?

    A. The inability to stem Confederate traffic through the city of Baltimore
    B. A lack of anticipation by the secretary of the navy
    C. A preoccupation with the blockade of Southern ports
    D. A reluctance to alienate the people of a state that had not yet declared secession

35. According to the beliefs of Andrew Johnson, which of the following had been Union goals for the prosecution of the Civil War?

    I. Preservation of the Union
    II. Emancipation
    III. The equal status of whites and free blacks

    The CORRECT answer is:

    A. I only
    B. I, II
    C. II only
    D. III only

36. During the early 1800s, even many Northerners were inhospitable to free blacks. In particular, immigrants from _____ were hostile to blacks, whom they viewed as wage-lowerers.

    A. Mexico   B. Poland   C. Ireland   D. Germany

37. In what year was the importation of slaves to the United States made illegal?

    A. 1787   B. 1808   C. 1848   D. 1865

38. Which of the following military commanders was NOT involved in the battle of Antietam?

    A. Ulysses S. Grant
    B. Robert E. Lee
    C. Thomas J. *Stonewall* Jackson
    D. George McClellan

39. The legacies of the reconstruction era of the United States generally include each of the following EXCEPT the

    A. emergence of the Federal government's precedence over states' rights
    B. rejection of complaints against majoritarianism in American government
    C. dominance of industrial over agrarian economic forces
    D. rejection of caste as the basis for the American social order

40. Which of the following cities was known to have strong Southern sympathies throughout the Civil War?

    A. New York   B. Boston
    C. Philadelphia   D. Chicago

41. Following an initial post-war slump, the economy in the North underwent a remarkable resurgence, which was most evident in the field of

    A. petroleum refining   B. railroad building
    C. home construction   D. steel processing

42. Which of the following factors best explains the cautious nature of President Lincoln's first military measures of the war?

    A. Inexperience in military matters
    B. The fear of suffering a major loss that could terminate the Northern numerical advantage
    C. The fear of sparking foreign interest in the cause of the South
    D. The fear of alienating border states

43. Which of the following Southern states seceded from the Union after the incident at Fort Sumter?

    A. Louisiana   B. Georgia
    C. Texas   D. North Carolina

44. Who was responsible for the 1863 sacking of Lawrence, Kansas and the later Massacre at Baxter Springs?

    A. James Blunt   B. Frank James
    C. John Robert Baylor   D. William Quantrill

45. The Republican Party in the United States was formed by a politically varied collection of people who were generally united in reaction against the   45._____

    A. Kansas-Nebraska Act   B. Fugitive Slave Act
    C. writ of habeas corpus   D. Gadsden Purchase

46. Most of the Quaker-operated *underground railroad stations* were located in the state of   46._____

    A. Iowa   B. Indiana
    C. Illinois   D. Tennessee

47. Abraham Lincoln's Democratic opponent in the election of 1864 was   47._____

    A. Clement Vallandigham   B. Benjamin Wade
    C. George McClellan   D. Salmon P. Chase

48. The common tactical infantry and cavalry unit of the Civil War was the   48._____

    A. company   B. brigade   C. regiment   D. corps

49. During his conduct of the Union war effort, Abraham Lincoln committed several violations   49._____
    of the United States Constitution, including
    I. suspension of the writ of habeas corpus
    II. military supervision of elections
    III. direct appropriation of advance funding from the Treasury for military purposes
    IV. increasing the size of the United States army without congressional approval
    The CORRECT answer is:

    A. I only   B. I, III, IV
    C. I, III   D. I, II, III, IV

50. What was the term used to denote civilians who were officially appointed to supply soldiers with a list of approved items such as food, cutlery, newspapers, and books?   50._____

    A. Contrabands   B. Factors
    C. Vivandieres   D. Sutlers

KEY (CORRECT ANSWERS)

1. D	11. C	21. D	31. D	41. B
2. C	12. B	22. D	32. C	42. D
3. B	13. C	23. A	33. C	43. D
4. D	14. A	24. C	34. D	44. D
5. D	15. B	25. C	35. B	45. A
6. D	16. B	26. D	36. C	46. A
7. C	17. D	27. C	37. B	47. C
8. C	18. B	28. B	38. A	48. B
9. D	19. C	29. B	39. B	49. D
10. B	20. B	30. C	40. A	50. D

TEST 4

DIRECTIONS: Each question or incomplete statement is followed by several suggested answers or completions. Select the one that BEST answers the question or completes the statement. *PRINT THE LETTER OF THE CORRECT ANSWER IN THE SPACE AT THE RIGHT.*

1. The first list of accusations against President Johnson that were investigated by Congress in 1867 a prelude to the coming impeachment process — included each of the following EXCEPT   1.____

    A. violation of the Tenure-of-Office Act
    B. corrupt use of veto and appointing powers
    C. complicity in the Lincoln assassination
    D. the pardon of Confederate officials and military personnel

2. Who was the Union Army's chief of staff at the outset of the Civil War?   2.____

    A. George McClellan B. Winfield Scott
    C. Benjamin Butler   D. Irvin McDowell

3. The stance of most antebellum *free-soilers* was that   3.____

    A. slavery should be abolished outright in the South
    B. slavery should be gradually phased out by individual Southern state legislatures
    C. the institution should not be abolished but should be prohibited in the territories
    D. nobody born within the United States should be a slave under any circumstances

4. The first battle of Bull Run was fought along a Confederate line of defense known as the   4.____

    A. Tar Meridian   B. Skein
    C. Alexandria Line   D. Lookout Ridge

5. In 1877, federal troops were finally withdrawn from the states of _____, as a result of the Hayes-Tilden electoral bargain.   5.____

    A. Louisiana and South Carolina
    B. Mississippi and Alabama
    C. North Carolina and South Carolina
    D. Florida and Georgia

6. Which of the following was a slave state throughout the Civil War?   6.____

    A. Missouri   B. Maryland
    C. West Virginia   D. Delaware

7. A(n) _____ can be said to have considerably prolonged the war for the North.   7.____

    A. over-reliance on naval superiority
    B. preoccupation with defeating General Lee and the Army of Northern Virginia
    C. underestimation of the Southern resolve
    D. failure to develop a coherent strategy on the Western front

8. Who commanded the Confederate Army of Tennessee in 1864?   8.____

    A. James Longstreet   B. Braxton Bragg
    C. Thomas J. *Stonewall* Jackson D. Joseph E. Johnston

83

9. After the war had ended, how many Confederates, excluding the Lincoln assassination conspirators, were eventually executed for the commission of war crimes?

   A. 0 B. 1 C. 7 D. 13

10. Throughout the war, the Confederate cabinet was served by at least one man from each of the following states EXCEPT

    A. South Carolina B. Tennessee
    C. Kentucky D. North Carolina

11. The general plan of Northern attack during the Civil War evolved to include four main elements. Which of the following was NOT one of these?

    A. Strangulation through the capture of Richmond
    B. Suffocation through blockade
    C. Bisection through control of the Mississippi River
    D. Penetration through control of the Shenandoah Valley

12. The Confederacy's gap in war materiel was closed in large part by the prodigious output of the powder works of George W. Rains at

    A. Raleigh, North Carolina B. Montgomery, Alabama
    C. Lynchburg, Virginia D. Augusta, Georgia

13. Who was the Whig candidate for president in the election of 1852?

    A. Daniel Webster B. Abraham Lincoln
    C. Franklin Pierce D. Winfield Scott

14. By 1863, it was estimated by the United States (Union) government that the Civil War was costing about _____ daily.

    A. $750,000 B. $1.2 million
    C. $2.5 million D. $4.6 million

15. While George McClellan was assuming command of the Army of the Potomac, Union forces suffered a defeat at _____, which resulted in the loss of General Nathaniel Lyon and the demotion of General John C. Fremont.

    A. Balls Bluff, Virginia B. Corinth, Mississippi
    C. Cairo, Illinois D. Wilson's Creek, Missouri

16. Each of the following was a trend in Southern life in the decades before the outbreak of war EXCEPT

    A. poor farmers accepted the status quo
    B. trained urban professionals switched to agriculture for reasons of social status
    C. the overall value of land decreased slightly
    D. the number of poor whites increased at a greater rate than that of slaveholding whites

17. At war's end, the most serious problems for the South were _____ in nature.

    A. economic B. political
    C. social D. psychological

18. The first Southern port to be blockaded by the north was _____, in 1861.

    A. Pensacola
    B. Charleston
    C. New Orleans
    D. Wilmington

19. The Southern cause of secession received open sympathy from the ruling classes of each of the following foreign countries EXCEPT

    A. France
    B. Russia
    C. Germany
    D. Great Britain

20. What was the term (in both the North and the South) for a unit of 50-100 soldiers commanded by a captain?

    A. Regiment   B. Company   C. Platoon   D. Brigade

21. The main idea of the fateful *Freeport Doctrine* expressed by Stephen Douglas during his debates with Abraham Lincoln was that

    A. the Supreme Court's Dred Scott decision was rightfully the law of the land
    B. territories should be allowed self-determination on the issue of slavery
    C. the sectional balance among states and territories should be preserved at all costs
    D. the Missouri Compromise never should have been invalidated

22. In the conflict known as *Bleeding Kansas*, who carried out the so-called 1856 Potawatomi Massacre?

    A. Dave Poole
    B. William Quantrill
    C. Frank James
    D. John Brown

23. When Northern lawmakers criticized the 1853 Gadsden Purchase of an area of land from Mexico, their complaints centered on the

    A. cost of the purchase in light of its apparent usefulness
    B. practice of slavery that was rumored to be in operation in the territory
    C. possibility of a land grab by Southern sectionalists
    D. circumvention of Senate approval

24. At the outbreak of the war, the leading abolitionist in the United States House of Representatives was

    A. Charles Francis Adams
    B. Thaddeus Stevens
    C. Sidney George Fisher
    D. Charles Sumner

25. The *Middle Phase* of the Civil War included each of the following battles EXCEPT

    A. Chattanooga
    B. Atlanta
    C. Vicksburg
    D. Gettysburg

26. The first anti-slavery political organization in the United States was the _____ Party, organized in 1840.

    A. Free Soil
    B. Free Chattel
    C. Liberty
    D. Know-Nothing

27. Which of the following newspapers was the leading anti-administration advocate of slavery and secession in the Southern United States? The.

 A. Columbia *South Carolinian*
 B. Charleston *Mercury*
 C. Baltimore *Sun*
 D. Kansas City *Star*

28. Probably the most important rendezvous point for Confederate blockade-runners throughout the Civil War was

 A. Havana
 B. Halifax
 C. Cape Hatteras
 D. Nassau

29. For what reason did foreign governments sympathetic to the Confederacy not attempt to break through the Northern blockade during the war?

 A. They did not want to risk a war with the Union.
 B. They thought it would constitute a violation of the Monroe Doctrine.
 C. They had an adequate corps of privateers to do the job for them.
 D. Popular sentiment in their countries was against them.

30. Which of the following served as secretary of war in the administration of Abraham Lincoln?

 A. Salmon P. Chase
 B. Simon Cameron
 C. Caleb Smith
 D. U.S. Grant

31. Approximately what percentage of Union forces throughout the war were volunteers?

 A. 35
 B. 60
 C. 75
 D. 90

32. The main platform of the Know-Nothing Party, which rose to prominence in the 1850s, was centered on the issue of

 A. the secret role of the Society of Freemasons in public life
 B. taxation
 C. the abolition of slavery
 D. immigration and foreign settlement

33. During the period of military reconstruction, who was responsible for implementing the reconstruction of South Carolina?

 A. Daniel Sickles
 B. John Pope
 C. John M. Schofield
 D. Edward Ord

34. The primary unit in the Union's Regular army was the

 A. brigade
 B. regiment
 C. division
 D. company

35. Which of the following battles is said to have opened the door to the mid-South for Union forces?

    A. Forts Henry and Donelson
    B. Murfreesboro
    C. Shiloh
    D. Vicksburg

36. In January of 1861, the flag of the *Pacific Republic* was raised in

    A. Astoria, by Oregon neutralists
    B. San Francisco, by pro-Union Californians
    C. San Diego, by defectors from the Union Navy
    D. Stockton, by pro-Confederate Californians

37. Which of the following Southern states was NOT subjected to military reconstruction after the war?

    A. Arkansas
    B. Virginia
    C. Tennessee
    D. North Carolina

38. Who commanded the Union Army of the James in the failed Bermuda Hundred campaign of 1864?

    A. Henry Halleck
    B. Benjamin Butler
    C. George Gordon Meade
    D. George McClellan

39. The sharecropping system that arose in the South after the Civil War had the effect of
    I. the replacement of factors with bankers as sources for capital
    II. the increasing Southern reliance on a limited number of crops
    III. a loss of control for the planter over the purchasing process
    The CORRECT answer is:

    A. I only
    B. I, III
    C. II only
    D. I, II, III

40. What was the term used throughout most of the war to denote slaves of indeterminate status who had been liberated by the military but could not yet be declared free?

    A. Foragers
    B. Collaterals
    C. Spoils
    D. Contrabands

41. In all of the antebellum South, by far the majority of Southerners were

    A. slaves
    B. poor whites
    C. rich planters
    D. small farmers

42. Each of the following cities was an important link in the Underground Railroad during the 1850s EXCEPT

    A. Pittsburgh
    B. Chicago
    C. Columbus
    D. Detroit

43. The corps known as Berdan's Sharpshooters made their greatest contribution to the Union military effort by protecting the Federal flank at the battle of

    A. Second Bull Run
    B. Antietam
    C. Gettysburg
    D. Shiloh

44. General Lee's goals for his Antietam Campaign included
    I. winning over the border states
    II. encouraging foreign intervention
    III. plowing a route to Washington

    The CORRECT answer is:

    A. I only   B. I, II   C. III only   D. II, III

45. What was the nickname given to the foragers who accompanied General William T. Sherman during his march to the sea and Carolinas campaign?

    A. Clinkers   B. Idlers
    C. Scroungers   D. Bummers

46. The value of United States *greenbacks* issued during the war was determined by

    A. the nation's credit   B. the British pound
    C. bond sales   D. the gold standard

47. The first Confederate invasion of the New Mexico territory was undertaken in 1861 as an ostensible *buffalo hunt,* led by

    A. Henry H. Sibley   B. John Robert Baylor
    C. Isaac Lynde   D. Sam Houston

48. In 1866, President Johnson vetoed a bill that would have renewed the authority of the Freedmen's Bureau. His primary reason for doing this was that

    A. freedmen were already being granted adequate protection under the new state governments
    B. it would constitute an unwarranted continuance of a war power in a time of peace
    C. it would have given too much power to his political adversaries in Congress
    D. freedmen were too susceptible to exploitation by officers

49. The *carpetbaggers* who occupied the South during and after the Civil War were most disproportionately numerous in the state of

    A. Arkansas   B. Alabama   C. Louisiana   D. Mississippi

50. Which of the following was NOT a founding member of the American Anti-Slavery Society?

    A. James G. Birney   B. Elijah Lovejoy
    C. Lewis Tappan   D. Theodore D. Weld

KEY (CORRECT ANSWERS)

1. A	11. D	21. B	31. D	41. D
2. B	12. D	22. D	32. D	42. A
3. C	13. D	23. A	33. A	43. C
4. C	14. C	24. B	34. D	44. B
5. A	15. D	25. B	35. A	45. D
6. D	16. C	26. C	36. D	46. A
7. B	17. A	27. B	37. C	47. B
8. D	18. A	28. D	38. B	48. B
9. B	19. B	29. D	39. D	49. D
10. B	20. B	30. B	40. D	50. B

EXAMINATION SECTION
TEST 1

DIRECTIONS: Each question or incomplete statement is followed by several suggested answers or completions. Select the one that BEST answers the question or completes the statement. *PRINT THE LETTER OF THE CORRECT ANSWER IN THE SPACE AT THE RIGHT.*

1. President Lincoln's reluctance to emancipate slaves in the first two years of the Civil War can most clearly be attributed to his

    A. uncertainty about the morality of slavery
    B. desire to retain the loyalty of border states
    C. uncertainty about the constitutionality of slavery
    D. fear of British and French intervention in the war

    1._____

2. Southern demands that slavery be allowed to expand into the western territories seems to have been motivated largely by the

    A. profiteering machinations of powerful agricultural interests
    B. desire for a wider market for surplus slaves
    C. fear that free territories would become breeding grounds for abolitionist agitators
    D. doctrine of paternalism, which held that slavery actually protected blacks

    2._____

3. The Civil Rights Act of 1866, passed over President Johnson's veto, granted African-Americans the right to
    I. make contracts
    II. own land and private property
    III. sue
    IV. vote

    A. I only
    B. I, II and III
    C. III only
    D. I, II, III and IV

    3._____

4. The Union victory that essentially split the Confederacy in half occurred at

    A. Atlanta
    B. Antietam
    C. Vicksburg
    D. Chattanooga

    4._____

5. When Ulysses S. Grant was made General-in-Chief of the Union armed forces, he
    I. abolished the exchange of prisoners
    II. concentrated Union forces in the West
    III. pressed southward after the battle of the Wilderness
    IV. decided upon a "war of attrition" strategy that was sure to produce many Union casualties

    A. I and II
    B. I, III and IV

    5._____

91

C. III and IV
D. I, II, III and IV

6. The term "Solid South" was applied to the former Confederate States after Reconstruction because these states

   A. passed a number of Jim Crow laws
   B. exhibited a culture that proved to be impenetrable to outsiders
   C. turned increasingly toward an industrial economy
   D. consistently voted Democratic

6.____

7. The Compromise of 1850 was approved by President

   A. James K. Polk
   B. Franklin Pierce
   C. Millard Fillmore
   D. Zachary Taylor

7.____

8. Which of the following Union generals declared in 1862 that slaves in the states of Georgia, South Carolina, and Florida were free by virtue of the states' subjection to martial law only to have the order promptly rescinded by President Lincoln?

   A. Philip Sheridan
   B. Benjamin Butler
   C. George Armstrong Custer
   D. David Hunter

8.____

9. In the first 25 years of the 19th century, the event that had the greatest impact on the institution of slavery was the

   A. increasing domestic demand for cotton from textile manufacturers
   B. invention of the cotton gin
   C. use of more repressive means of discipline
   D. introduction of crop rotation and fertilizers

9.____

10. "Fire-Eaters" were

    A. extreme abolitionists who, like John Brown, advocated emancipation through violence
    B. Northern politicians who traveled South to make their fortune during Reconstruction
    C. extremist pro-slavery politicians from the South
    D. Union Navy personnel who took on the dangerous job of loading onboard cannons with balls and shot

10.____

11. Which of the following parties, in the decade before the Civil War, generally supported Western expansion, a strong federal government, and the abolition of slavery?

    A. Democratic
    B. Know-Nothing
    C. Repuliican
    D. Free Soil

11.____

12. The overarching intent of Union General Winfield Scott's "Anaconda Plan" was to win the war   12.____

    A. rapidly by capturing the Confederate capital
    B. by draining escaped slaves away from the South and putting them to work
    C. with minimal bloodshed
    D. by ruining the South's capability to fight

13. Each of the following battles was a part of the Overland Campaign, EXCEPT   13.____

    A. Cold Harbor
    B. Gettysburg
    C. Wilson's Wharf
    D. Spotsylvania

14. As president, James Buchanan urged that the issues related to slavery in the territories should be decided by   14.____

    A. armed conflict
    B. a national referendum
    C. the Supreme Court
    D. popular sovereignty

15. The Militia Act of 1862 decreed that all freed slaves could   15.____

    A. enlist in the Union military service, but only as laborers, not as soldiers.
    B. be drafted in the Union military service, but would only perform labor.
    C. enlist in the Union military service and move up the ranks through promotion, like any other soldier
    D. enlist in the Union military service but not serve as officers in any capacity

16. Juneteenth is an official holiday, celebrated in more than a dozen U.S. states, that commemorates the announcement of the abolition of slavery in   16.____

    A. Georgia
    B. Mississippi
    C. Florida
    D. Texas

17. The "fifth border state," carved out of pro-union slave territory, was   17.____

    A. Delaware
    B. West Virginia
    C. Indiana
    D. Tennessee

18. The Radical Republicans' extension of the vote to freedmen in the Southern states was   18.____

    A. grantee, because without black suffrage, the states would not ratify the Fourteenth Amendment
    B. widely perceived as a cynical ploy to secure millions of voters as Republicans for years to come

C. from the beginning, one of the most basic requirements of a Southern state's readmission to the Union
D. an attempt to stave off the effects of the "black codes"

19. The _____ Amendment to the Constitution provides equality before the law and citizenship rights to African-Americans.

    A. Twelfth
    B. Thirteenth
    C. Fourteenth
    D. Fifteenth

20. One important reason that the Radical Republicans began to lose power was that

    A. Southern states were not making any substantial progress toward providing civil liberties for freed slaves
    B. they suffered from internal squabbles that divided their political strength
    C. many Northerners lost interest in changing the South
    D. they opposed the imperial expansion of U.S. power overseas, which was becoming an increasingly popular idea

21. The Confederate general who advocated the establishment of permanent "entrenched" lines of defense against Union invasion, and who thus presaged the advent of trench warfare, was

    A. Thomas J. "Stonewall" Jackson
    B. Robert E. Lee
    C. J.E.B. Stuart
    D. Braxton Bragg.

22. The primary reason for the exclusion of free blacks from the Union Army during the early stages of the Civil War was that

    A. most Northerners were opposed to blacks serving in the Army
    B. most white soldiers refused to serve with blacks
    C. it was against federal law to arm black people
    D. at the time, the North already had sufficient troops

23. During the Civil War, the Union objective that proved to be the most difficult, and which took the longest to achieve, was the

    A. naval blockade of Southern ports
    B. control of Mississippi River traffic
    C. capture of New Orleans
    D. capture of Richmond

24. The position of most American black leaders regarding the resettlement plan proposed by the American Colonization Society in the early 19th century was that they were

    A. opposed to it because they felt attached to the United States
    B. opposed to it because they considered it a scheme to deport free blacks
    C. in favor of it because ex-slaves would receive both land and material provisions
    D. in favor of it because ex-slaves would finally have the right to self-determination

25. U.S. territories that sided with the Confederacy during the Civil War included 25.____
    I. Montana
    II. Colorado
    III. Indian Territory (Oklahoma)
    IV. New Mexico

    A. I and II
    B. I and III
    C. III and IV
    D. None of the above

KEY (CORRECT ANSWERS)

1. B
2. C
3. B
4. C
5. B

6. D
7. C
8. D
9. B
10. C

11. C
12. C
13. B
14. C
15. A

16. D
17. B
18. A
19. C
20. C

21. B
22. C
23. D
24. B
25. C

TEST 2

DIRECTIONS: Each question or incomplete statement is followed by several suggested answers or completions. Select the one that BEST answers the question or completes the statement. *PRINT THE LETTER OF THE CORRECT ANSWER IN THE SPACE AT THE RIGHT.*

1. President Lincoln's justification for the Civil War could best be summed up by the statement that

    A. the Northern states were entitled share the resources of Southern states
    B. he was an abolitionist who wanted to end slavery in the United States
    C. his oath of office required that he work to defend and preserve the Union
    D. his constitutional authority required that he punish rebellion

    1.____

2. What was the post-Reconstruction case in which the U.S. Supreme Court ruled that "separate but equal" public facilities for black and white Americans were lawful?

    A. *Plessy v. Ferguson*
    B. *Giles v. Harris*
    C. *Dred Scott v. Sandford*
    D. *Civil Rights Cases (1883)*

    2.____

3. The Free Soil Party was formed in the United States largely as a faction in support of the

    A. Missouri Compromise
    B. Wilmot Proviso
    C. Kansas-Nebraska Act
    D. Emancipation Proclamation

    3.____

4. The Compromise of 1850 could most accurately be described as a series of laws that were intended to

    A. clarify some of the vagueness inherent in the doctrine of "popular sovereignty"
    B. increase Northern political control over the western territories
    C. stem the violence in "Bleeding Kansas"
    D. resolve sectional and territorial issues arising from the Mexican-American War

    4.____

5. Which of the following occurred FIRST?

    A. Peninsula campaign (March-July 1862)
    B. Siege of Petersburg
    C. Gettysburg
    D. Chickamauga

    5.____

6. How many slave uprisings in the antebellum South resulted in the death of whites?

    A. 1
    B. 2
    C. 4
    D. 7

    6.____

7. President Lincoln's plan for Reconstruction required Southern states to
    I. guarantee suffrage for blacks
    II. adopt a republican form of government
    III. require some Southerners to take an oath of loyalty to the Union
    IV. accept the abolition of slavery

    A. I and IV
    B. IV only
    C. II, III and IV
    D. I, II, III and IV

8. The _____ was an overt statement that African-Americans could never be citizens of the United States.

    A. *Dred Scott* decision
    B. Compromise of 1820
    C. Lecompton Constitution
    D. Fugitive Slave Law

9. During the first half of the 19th century, the most divisive and controversial issue regarding slavery was the status of

    A. the international slave trade
    B. slavery in the District of Columbia
    C. slavery in the western territories
    D. fugitive slaves

10. The most strategically important location to be captured by the Union Navy during the first year of the war was

    A. New Orleans
    B. Savannah
    C. Port Royal
    D. Wilmington

11. Which of the following black abolitionists was arguably the first proponent of American black nationalism and the first African American field officer in the U.S. Army?

    A. Martin Delaney
    B. David Walker
    C. Frederick Douglass
    D. Elijah Lovejoy

12. For blacks who fled the South during the Reconstruction Era, the two most likely destinations were:

    A. New York (Harlem) and Philadelphia
    B. Detroit and Chicago
    C. Canada and Cuba
    D. Kansas and Liberia

13. The name given those settlers in Kansas Territory during the 1850s "Bleeding Kansas" era who opposed the extension of slavery into Kansas was

A. Jay hawkers
B. Leavenworths
C. Free Staters
D. Thayerites

14. The National Union Party came to an end when

   A. George McClellan was defeated
   B. Abraham Lincoln was assassinated
   C. Ulysses S. Grant was elected president
   D. Andrew Johnson's term ended

15. Men who enlisted in the Union Army in 1861 signed up for a period of

   A. eight months
   B. one year
   C. eighteen months
   D. three years

16. By 1860, _____ , which had no railroads in 1850, had twelve lines running through it.

   A. New York City
   B. Columbus
   C. Chicago
   D. Kansas City

17. At the outset of the Civil War, the North had a numerical advantage over the South in each of the following, EXCEPT

   A. taxable wealth
   B. West Point graduates
   C. existing capital
   D. industrial capacity

18. During the Civil War, Winston County, in the state of _____ refused to join the Confederacy and declared itself the Republic of Winston.

   A. Missouri
   B. Alabama
   C. Virginia
   D. Florida

19. President Andrew Johnson's narrow avoidance of conviction on impeachment charges was largely due to

   A. several compromises worked out in secret to appease the Radical Republican faction that sought his removal
   B. his agreement to backtrack and reappoint his secretary of war
   C. the reluctance of some Republicans to use impeachment as a political weapon against the presidency
   D. the moral authority he carried as Abraham Lincoln's choice for the vice presidency

20. Which of the following, killed relatively early in the Civil War at Shiloh, was considered by Jefferson Davis to be the finest general in the Confederacy?

   A. J.E.B. Stuart
   B. Albert Sidney Johnston
   C. Braxton Bragg
   D. Thomas J. "Stonewall" Jackson

21. Slavery was abolished in the United States by the _____ Amendment to the Constitution.

   A. Twelfth
   B. Thirteenth
   C. Fourteenth
   D. Fifteenth

22. *I am not now, nor ever have been in favor of bringing about in any way the social or political equality of the white and black races. I am not now nor ever have been in favor of making voters or jurors of Negroes, nor of qualifying them to hold office, nor of intermarriages with white people. There is a physical difference between the white and the black races which will forever forbid the two races living together on social or political equality. There must be a position of superior and inferior, and I am in favor of assigning the superior position to the white man.*

   The words above were spoken in 1858 by

   A. Jefferson Davis
   B. Abraham Lincoln
   C. John C. Calhoun
   D. Stephen A. Douglas

23. During the Civil War the North experienced several riots sparked by the issue of _____ and the South suffered riots over the issue of _____.

   A. slavery; secession
   B. popular sovereignty; the enlistment of blacks in the Confederate Army
   C. British meddling; the fugitive slave laws
   D. the military draft; food

24. During the Civil War, Great Britain and France generally

   A. saw advantages in a divided United States, but pursued cautious policies toward both sides
   B. favored permanent separation, but openly supported the North
   C. supported the South, despite their opposition to slavery, because of their dependence on Southern cotton
   D. had no interest in the outcome of the conflict

25. Regarding free black people in the antebellum United States,
    I. most preferred to live in cities
    II. some owned property, and a few owned slaves
    III. some who owned property could vote
    IV. some were kidnapped and sold into slavery in another state

    A. I only
    B. I, II and IV
    C. II and III
    D. I, II, III and IV

KEY (CORRECT ANSWERS)

1.	C	11.	A
2.	A	12.	D
3.	B	13.	C
4.	D	14.	D
5.	A	15.	D
6.	A	16.	A
7.	C	17.	B
8.	A	18.	B
9.	C	19.	C
10.	C	20.	B

21. B
22. B
23. D
24. A
25. B

TEST 3

DIRECTIONS: Each question or incomplete statement is followed by several suggested answers or completions. Select the one that BEST answers the question or completes the statement. *PRINT THE LETTER OF THE CORRECT ANSWER IN THE SPACE AT THE RIGHT.*

1. What was the term used for pro-Union guerilla fighters in the Kansas Territory during the Civil War?   1._____

    A. Jay hawkers
    B. Bushwhackers
    C. Butternuts
    D. Hedge-apples

2. General Benjamin Butler's insistence that escaped slaves should be freed was based on the   2._____

    A. dire shortage of Union troops, which could be alleviated by the use of black troops
    B. principle that slavery was a moral evil
    C. unsolvable question of whether they were slaves or kidnapped free blacks
    D. fact that once returned to their masters, they were effectively aiding the Confederacy

3. Pickett's Charge, the infamous assault ordered by General Robert E. Lee that killed more than half the Confederate troops who carried it out, occurred at the Battle of   3._____

    A. Gettysburg
    B. Chancellors ville
    C. Antietam
    D. Spotsylvania

4. The Reconstruction proposal offered by Andrew Johnson included each of the following, EXCEPT   4._____

    A. full civil and political equality for freed blacks
    B. allowing Southern states to adopt special legal codes
    C. increasing the number of Democrats in Congress
    D. allowing former Confederate officials to hold office

5. Which of the following events occurred LAST?   5._____

    A. Compromise of 1850
    B. Crittenden Compromise
    C. Firing on Fort Sumter
    D. Crittenden-Johnson Resolution

6. The *Dred Scott* decision seemed to indicate that   6._____

    A. the Constitution's position of slavery was clear
    B. most Supreme Court justices sympathized with the South
    C. most Supreme Court justices had become impatient with the issue of slavery and wanted it to become more settled
    D. the American press generally supported slavery

7. The election of 1860 resulted in each of the following, EXCEPT

   A. the Democratic Party dividing into feuding Northern and Southern wings
   B. the splintering of the Republican Party over the issue of slavery
   C. the President of the United States had virtually no support in the South
   D. an election winner who was chosen by less than half the population

8. Most northerners who voiced opposition to the extension of slavery into the western territories did so on the grounds that

   A. slavery was immoral
   B. free workers would be forced to compete with slaves for jobs
   C. it would create a sectional imbalance in the legislature
   D. slavery inevitably ushered in higher taxes and a more regulated economy

9. The only major candidate in the election of 1860 who seemed to believe that secession was a real possibility was

   A. William Seward
   B. Abraham Lincoln
   C. John Bell
   D. Stephen Douglas

10. The Union advance to Vicksburg was enabled by the victory at

    A. Shiloh
    B. Jackson
    C. Antietam
    D. New Orleans

11. Southern whites who supported Reconstruction in the South were typically referred to as

    A. Fire-Eaters
    B. redeemers
    C. carpetbaggers
    D. scalawags

12. The short-lived Know-Nothing Party was promptly undone by the issue of _____ and disappeared from American politics.

    A. immigiation
    B. slavery
    C. federal funding for internal improvements
    D. temperance

13. The Union Victory at _____ was strategically important because it secured control of the entire Mississippi River.

    A. Hannibal
    B. Memphis
    C. New Orleans
    D. Vicksburg

14. Of the following, the event that occurred FIRST was 14.____

    A. The enactment of the Fugitive Slave Law
    B. The formation of the Liberty Party
    C. William Lloyd Garrison's publication of *The Liberator*
    D. The C mpromise of 1850

15. The use of slave labor in colonial Virginia 15.____

    A. fulfilled the original plan of the Virginia Company
    B. spread rapidly as blacks displaced white indentured servants
    C. was forced onto reluctant Virginians by English merchants and the Crown
    D. was the first instance of European enslavement of Africans

16. The percentage of Southern officeholders who were African-American during the Reconstruction era was about 16.____

    A. 5
    B. 20
    C. 45
    D. 60

17. Southern support for the Compromise of 1850 was based primarily on its provision for 17.____

    A. an equal number of free and slave states
    B. the possibility of Texas being divided into five separate states
    C. slavery in all newly acquired territories
    D. the return of fugitive slaves

18. Each of the following battles was a victory for General Ulysses S. Grant, EXCEPT 18.____

    A. Chickamauga
    B. Shiloh
    C. Chattanooga
    D. Fort Donelson

19. The Civil Rights Act of 1866 was vetoed by President Andrew Johnson on the grounds that it 19.____

    A. would operate in favor of the black race and against the white race
    B. would further divide Northern and Southern states
    C. was unconstitutional
    D. did noi go far enough in granting civil liberties to freed slaves

20. Ultimately, the legislative battle over the impeachment of President Andrew Johnson was fought over the constitutional principle of 20.____

    A. the "three-fifths" rule
    B. separation of powers
    C. interstate commerce
    D. free speech and assembly

21. In 1852, Whig candidate Winfield Scott

    A. urged the Supreme Court to settle the issue of slavery once and for all
    B. would likely have won the election if he hadn't supported a high tariff
    C. ran on a platform that called for popular sovereignty in the territories
    D. alienated Southern voters by aligning himself with Northern anti-slavery leaders

22. The constitution that finally settled the issue of slavery in Kansas was the _____ Constitution, adopted in 1858 and establishing it as a free state

    A. Topeka
    B. Leavenworth
    C. Wyandotte
    D. Lecompton

23. Radical and moderate Republicans united in opposition to President Andrew Johnson after his

    A. dismissal of Secretary of War Edwin Stanton
    B. vetoes of the Freedmen's Bureau bill and the Civil Rights Act
    C. refusal to deviate from Abraham Lincoln's plan for Reconstruction
    D. proposal for a federal agency to provide relief, food and medical care to poor white Southerners

24. The 1858 Lincoln-Douglas debates for the Senate seat from Illinois focused primanly on the issue of

    A. states' rights
    B. monetary policy
    C. slavery
    D. tariffs

25. The newly formed Republican Party achieved rapid prosperity

    A. with its first national ticket
    B. because of its advocacy of popular sovereignty in the territories
    C. because of outrage over "Bleeding Kansas" and the caning of Senator Charles Sumner
    D. in the South in the elections of 1854

KEY (CORRECT ANSWERS)

1. A
2. D
3. A
4. A
5. D

6. B
7. B
8. B
9. D
10. A

11. D
12. B
13. D
14. C
15. B

16. B
17. D
18. A
19. A
20. B

21. D
22. C
23. C
24. C
25. C

TEST 4

DIRECTIONS: Each question or incomplete statement is followed by several suggested answers or completions. Select the one that BEST answers the question or completes the statement. *PRINT THE LETTER OF THE CORRECT ANSWER IN THE SPACE AT THE RIGHT.*

1. Which of the following was NOT a tactic used by abolitionists before the Civil War?

    A. Requesting that Congress pass laws outlawing slavery in the states
    B. Providing assistance to escaped slaves
    C. Appealing to the morality and conscience of slaveholders
    D. Lobbying state legislatures to pass personal liberty laws

    1.____

2. One direct result of the Fourteenth Amendment was that

    A. former slaves were given allotments of land by the federal government
    B. Southern states began to enact Jim Crow laws
    C. the Reconstruction Era had effectively come to an end
    D. the guarantees contained in the Bill of Rights were applied to all state actions

    2.____

3. President Buchanan considered the Lecompton Constitution to be a

    A. fundamentally flawed document that had no constitutional foundation
    B. violation of the principle of popular sovereignty
    C. sign that secession was imminent
    D. fairly moderate compromise that deserved to be adopted

    3.____

4. The Reconstruction-era political coalition known as the "Redeemers" was composed mostly of

    A. Bourbon Democrats
    B. carpetbaggers
    C. copperheads
    D. scalawags

    4.____

5. The _____ Party, formed in 1860, was made up of conservative Whigs who wanted to preserve the Union.

    A. Constitutional Union
    B. Free Soil
    C. Northern Democratic
    D. Know-Nothing

    5.____

6. Which of the following occurred LAST?

    A. Veto of Freedmen's Bureau extension
    B. Lincoln assassination
    C. Military Reconstruction Acts
    D. Johnson impeachment

    6.____

7. The Union Army expedition in the Mississippi Campaign was commanded by each of the following, EXCEPT

    A. Benjamin Butler
    B. Henry Halleck
    C. Nathaniel P. Banks
    D. Ulysses S. Grant

8. The Reconstruction Acts of 1867 applied to every Southern state except _____, which had ratified the Fourteenth Amendment.

    A. Alabama
    B. Virginia
    C. Texas
    D. Tennessee

9. Ulysses S. Grant's main competition for the presidency in the election of 1872 was

    A. Thomas Andrews Hendricks
    B. Rutherford B. Hayes
    C. William McKinley
    D. Horace Greeley

10. During the Civil War, Republicans enacted each of the following, EXCEPT

    A. land grants for railroad construction
    B. a low tariff to encourage free trade
    C. a national banking system
    D. free land to homesteaders

11. The Whig Party was essentially destroyed by the

    A. Kansas-Nebraska Act
    B. election of Abraham Lincoln
    C. annexation of Texas
    D. Missouri Compromise

12. The North effectively took control of the South's railroad network with the 1864 capture of

    A. Gettysburg
    B. Vicksburg
    C. Birmingham
    D. Atlanta

13. A white Southerner would be legally exempted from military duty if he

    A. filed for conscientious objector status
    B. received an educational deferment
    C. owned at least 20 slaves
    D. could prove he was the sole means of support for his dependents

14. Black politicians of the Reconstruction era tended to believe that

    A. none of the white race could be trusted
    B. it was only possible to work with Northern whites

C. blacks and Southern whites would have to find a way to work together
D. the only way for blacks to be safe was to establish isolated home-rule communities

15. The Union occupation of New Orleans was administered by

   A. David Farragut
   B. William Jennings Bryan
   C. Benjamin Butler
   D. Nathaniel P. Banks

16. The anti-abolitionist riots, also known as the Farren Riots, occurred in 1934 in the city of

   A. Richmond
   B. New York
   C. Charleston
   D. Philadelphia

17. Each of the following states seceded in 1861, as a direct result of President Lincoln's call for Union troops, EXCEPT

   A. Tennessee
   B. Texas
   C. Virginia
   D. Arkansas

18. *There are few, I believe, in this enlightened age, who will not acknowledge that slavery as an institution is a moral and political evil.*
    The words above were written by

   A. Alexander Stephens
   B. John C. Calhoun
   C. Robert E. Lee
   D. Abraham Lincoln

19. By the end of the first year of the Civil War, inflation in the Confederacy had reached a rate of _____ per month.

   A. 1
   B. 5
   C. 12
   D. 23

20. Which of the following NOT was a border state during the Civil War?

   A. Maryland
   B. Missouri
   C. West Virginia
   D. Tennessee

21. The Democratic nominee for president in the 1848 was a major proponent of popular sovereignty named

   A. Zachany Taylor
   B. George Dallas

C. James K. Polk
D. Lewis Cass

22. The pro-slavery guerillas who harassed the abolitionist settlements in "Bleeding Kansas" were known as

    A. Sunflowers
    B. Border Ruffians
    C. the James Gang
    D. Jayhawkers

23. The first major military clash of the Civil War occurred at

    A. Fort Sumter
    B. Stones River (Murfreesboro)
    C. Bull Run (Manassas)
    D. Gettysburg

24. Which of the following parties, in the decade before the Civil War, generally supported Western expansion, popular sovereignty, and states' rights?

    A. Democratic
    B. Republican
    C. Free Soil
    D. Whig

25. Which of the following terms was NOT commonly used to denote Northern Democrats who wanted to make peace with the South?

    A. Know-Nothings
    B. Copperheads
    C. Bushwhackers
    D. Butternuts

KEY (CORRECT ANSWERS)

1. A
2. D
3. D
4. A
5. A

6. D
7. A
8. D
9. D
10. B

11. A
12. D
13. C
14. C
15. C

16. B
17. B
18. C
19. C
20. D

21. D
22. B
23. C
24. A
25. B

EXAMINATION SECTION
TEST 1

DIRECTIONS: Each question or incomplete statement is followed by several suggested answers or completions. Select the one that BEST answers the question or completes the statement. *PRINT THE LETTER OF THE CORRECT ANSWER IN THE SPACE AT THE RIGHT.*

1. Sectional differences developed in the United States largely as a result of

    A. economic conditions and interests
    B. foreign subversion, especially on the part of Great Britain and France
    C. differences in ethnic and cultural patterns of settlement and migration
    D. the federal government's willingness to defer to the doctrine of states' rights

    1.____

2. The three-day Battle of _____ effectively saved the Union and permanently changed the course of the Civil War.

    A. Vicksburg
    B. Atlanta
    C. Shiloh
    D. Gettysburg

    2.____

3. By far, most of the military engagements between the North and the South during the Civil War took place in

    A. Tennessee
    B. Georgia
    C. South Carolina
    D. Virginia

    3.____

4. The poll taxes and literacy tests, and segregated facilities that were legally implemented in Southern states beginning in the post-Reconstruction era were examples of

    A. Jim Crow laws
    B. fugitive slave laws
    C. Black Codes
    D. civil rights laws

    4.____

5. The Military Reconstruction Act of 1867 provided for
    I. black suffrage in all Southern states
    II. the denial of suffrage to former Confederate officials and military officers
    III. military rule of the South
    IV. a ban on poll taxes and literacy tests

    A. I and II
    B. I, II and III
    C. II, III and IV
    D. I, II, III and IV

    5.____

6. Jefferson Davis's fundamental problem in leading the Confederate States of America was that

    6.____

111

A. in order to lead effectively, he had to seek more centralized authority over a society that valued states' rights
B. the war required a rapid mobilization that could not be conducted successfully in the South, because the infrastructure was so poorly conceived and maintained
C. there were not enough young Southern men dedicated to the cause of the Confederacy
D. he was a lofty, ideological thinker in a society that needed quick, pragmatic answers to mostly military questions

7. Fort Henry's strategic important was that it protected the

   A. Mobile Bay
   B. Ohio River Valley
   C. Biloxi Harbor
   D. Tennessee River

8. The Wilmot Proviso, if passed in 1846, would have

   A. left the issue of slavery in any territory acquired as a result of the Mexican War to be decided by popular sovereignty
   B. permitted slavery in any territory acquired as a result of the Mexican War
   C. banned slavery in any territory acquired as a result of the Mexican War
   D. banned slavery in all existing U.S. territories

9. Abraham Lincoln's military strategy could best be described as a(n)

   A. quick strike at the capital of Richmond that would precipitate the fall of the Confederacy
   B. grinding push to "clear and hold" the major urban centers
   C. two-front strategy that would keep pressure on Richmond while advancing in the Mississippi Valley
   D. "Anaconda Plan" of slowly starving the South into submission

10. The two Southern counties won by Lincoln during the 1860 election were in the state of

    A. Alabama
    B. Missouri
    C. Maryland
    D. Tennessee

11. The "Seven Days Battles" were fought in 1862 near

    A. Vicksburg
    B. Richmond
    C. Atlanta
    D. the Shenandoah Valley

12. The American Anti-Slavery Society was officially formed in

    A. 1789
    B. 1804
    C. 1833
    D. 1840

13. Specifically, the Freeport Doctrine argued that

    A. slavery could be prevented from any territory by the refusal of the people living in that territory to pass laws favorable to slavery
    B. slavery could not legally be extended into the territories
    C. the issue of slavery in the territories should be decided by popular sovereignty
    D. the international slave trade would soon die out if it were unregulated

14. Initially, the Emancipation Proclamation affected

    A. about 4 million slaves in the border states
    B. all slaves in the states that were loyal to the Union
    C. only those slaves that had already escaped to the Union side
    D. only those slaves whose freedom had been purchased by abolitionist activists

15. Southern Whigs' support of Zachary Taylor for the presidency in 1848 was due to his

    A. espousal of the doctrine of popular sovereignty
    B. support of the expansion of slavery into the territories
    C. outstanding record as a military hero during the Mexican-American War
    D. vocal support of the institution of slavery

16. The main reason that manufacturing in the South lagged behind that of the North was because

    A. white Southerners tended to look down on manufacturing jobs
    B. Southerners were generally less educated
    C. slave labor and industry were seen as incompatible
    D. cotton was more profitable

17. During the first year of the Civil War, about _____ of Confederate ships were able to penetrate the Union blockade.

    A. 90
    B. 65
    C. 35
    D. 10

18. In order to provide a haven for freed slaves during Reconstruction, President Ulysses S. Grant attempted to

    A. create legislation that would offer freedmen more favorable home-steading terms than whites
    B. elevate the Freedmen's Bureau to cabinet status
    C. set aside the recently unorganized territory of the Red River Valley as a "blacks only" settlement
    D. annex the Dominican Republic

19. During the Civil War, the South suffered shortages of each of the following, EXCEPT

    A. munitions
    B. food
    C. soldiers
    D. transportation facilities

20. Virginia's main pre-Civil War crop was

    A. tobacco
    B. hemp
    C. sugar
    D. cotton

21. Before the Civil War, abolitionists were generally unpopular among Northern business owners, because

    A. many Northern businesses depended on cotton from the South
    B. in their opinion, slaves were treated better than most Northern workers
    C. many Northerners still owned slaves who worked in factories
    D. the attacks and demonstrations by abolitionists tended to be violent and indiscriminate and often targeted business establishments

22. Which of the following cities was captured the day after the Battle of Gettysburg?

    A. Atlanta
    B. Fredericksburg
    C. Vicksburg
    D. Nashville

23. In the South, and especially Virginia, the Nat Turner rebellion and the publication of *The Liberator* had the effect of

    A. dividing Southerners among three clear-cut factions of abolitionists, moderates, and pro-slavery advocates
    B. encouraging state legislatures to discuss the issue of abolition in Congress
    C. galvanizing continued support for slavery
    D. encouraging the migration of slaves to the Midwest.

24. In 1858, when future President Abraham Lincoln said, "A house divided cannot stand," he indicated his belief that

    A. secession of the Southern states would be the most peaceful solution to the problem of slavery
    B. he intended to invade the South and free the slaves
    C. there should be a separate representative legislature for the South
    D. the nation could no longer exist as half slave and half free

25. Earlier efforts to settle the issue of slavery were frustrated in the 1840s and 1850s largely because

    A. the nation was expanding rapidly westward
    B. political parties were seizing on the issue as a "wedge" to divide the electorate and force them into political affiliations
    C. the Southern economy was nearing a collapse
    D. the British and French governments were sending agitators to the South

KEY (CORRECT ANSWERS)

1. A
2. D
3. D
4. A
5. B

6. A
7. D
8. C
9. C
10. B

11. B
12. C
13. A
14. C
15. B

16. D
17. A
18. D
19. A
20. A

21. A
22. C
23. C
24. D
25. A

TEST 2

DIRECTIONS: Each question or incomplete statement is followed by several suggested answers or completions. Select the one that BEST answers the question or completes the statement. *PRINT THE LETTER OF THE CORRECT ANSWER IN THE SPACE AT THE RIGHT.*

1. The _____ created a line at 3630'N to divide future slave and free territories and states in the United States. 1._____

   A. Missouri Compromise of 1820
   B. Compromise of 1850
   C. Fugitive Slave Act of 1850
   D. Kansas-Nebraska Act of 1854

2. Of the four proposed constitutions for the new state of Kansas, the _____ Constitution supported the existence of slavery in the proposed state and protected rights of slaveholders. 2._____

   A. Topeka
   B. Leavenworth
   C. Wyandotte
   D. Lecompton

3. The Confederate cavalry was commanded by 3._____

   A. J.E.B. Stuart
   B. Braxton Bragg
   C. Jubal Early
   D. P.G.T. Beauregard

4. The limited success of the Union's early eastern campaigns are most often attributed to 4._____

   A. the strategic brilliance of Confederate General
   B. George McClellan's overly cautious approach
   C. military genius of Robert E. Lee
   D. President Lincoln's constant interference in military matters

5. A major secessionist leader was 5._____

   A. Andrew Jackson
   B. William Yancey
   C. John Crittenden
   D. Robert E. Lee

6. In the United States, the principle of "popular sovereignty" 6._____
   I. was intended to be ambiguous
   II. was interpreted differently by Northerners and Southerners
   III. led to violence in the settlement of Kansas
   IV. was first codified in the Compromise of 1850

   A. I only
   B. I and III

C. II, III and IV
D. I, II, III and IV

7. Each of the following Civil War battles took place in Virginia, EXCEPT

    A. Games' Mill
    B. Bull Run
    C. Albemarle Sound
    D. Spotsylvania

8. Which of the following African-Americans called Reconstruction a "failure" because it did not follow through and reinforce the gains made by blacks in terms of civil and political rights?

    A. Booker T. Washington
    B. Frederick Douglass
    C. W.E.B. DuBois
    D. Harriet Beecher Stowe

9. Lincoln's pocket veto of the Wade-Davis Bill was motivated primarily by his desire to

    A. marginalize the Radicals in shaping Reconstruction policy
    B. keep Jefferson Davis from grasping for power in the legislature
    C. preserve the delicate political coalitions that he had begun to construct between northern and southern moderates
    D. ensure that Confederate leaders were properly punished for their role in starting the Civil War

10. The new political party formed in 1854 was the _____ Party.

    A. Bull Moose
    B. Know-Nothing
    C. Republican
    D. Free Soil

11. The Pinckney Resolutions that were passed in Congress in 1835 and renewed substantially for several ensuing years resulted in

    A. a tenuous sectional balance in the Senate, but not the House
    B. a limited ability for state governments to regulate slavery
    C. the rise of the "Fire-Eaters" among representatives from Southern states
    D. any petition regarding the issue of slavery to be tabled (neither read nor discussed)

12. The North tended to view the Reconstruction-era "black codes" as

    A. evidence that the South was slowly allowing freed slaves to improve their standing
    B. evidence that the South wanted to keep freed slaves economically dependent and legally inferior
    C. a dangerous experiment in Southern social engineering that would lead to the establishment of an extensive welfare state
    D. a pragmatic legislative solution to the problems posed in the South by the sudden influx of freed slaves into civil society

13. The "Peace Democrat" who was arrested and deported for treason by Abraham Lincoln was

    A. Daniel Voorhees
    B. Clement Vallandigham
    C. George McClellan
    D. Lambdin P. Milligan

13._____

14. A major factor in the increasing prosperity of the United States during the early 1850s was

    A. widespread foreclosures
    B. high tariffs
    C. the increasing amount of gold in the economy
    D. easy credit and widespread land speculation

14._____

15. President Andrew Johnson's plan for Reconstruction called for Southern states to

    A. declare that their secessions were illegal
    B. grant suffrage to former slaves
    C. pay war reparations
    D. ratify the Fourteenth Amendment

15._____

16. At the time the Emancipation Proclamation was issued, Lincoln's justification for it was the

    A. Union's military advantage
    B. economic benefits it would bring to the North
    C. constitutional guarantees of personal liberty
    D. moral imperative of ending slavery

16._____

17. Early in his presidency, Abraham Lincoln announced that the primary goal of his administration would be to

    A. abolish slavery throughout the country
    B. preserve the Union
    C. destroy the Southern plantation economy
    D. prevent slavery from extending into the western territories

17._____

18. The Civil War battle that resulted in the greatest number of casualties was

    A. Gettysburg
    B. Chancellorsville
    C. Shiloh
    D. Antietam

18._____

19. *This is to be a long war–very long – much longer than any politician thinks.* The words above were written in 1861 by

    A. Jefferson Davis
    B. William T. Sherman
    C. Frederick Douglass
    D. Abraham Lincoln

19._____

20. In January of 1862, Thaddeus Stevens, the Republican Leader in the House of Representatives, called for total war against the South, and argued that emancipation   20.____

    A. would win valuable black recruits to the Union Army
    B. was a moral imperative
    C. was a necessary step that would win international support
    D. would ruin the Southern economy

21. During Reconstruction, Congressional blacks such as Hiram Revels and Blanche K. Bruce advocated strongly for citizenship and suffrage for Indians and Chinese immigrants because they   21.____

    A. felt it was the only right thing to do, given their own record of persecution
    B. had designs on reservation lands as a haven for freedmen
    C. hoped to form a political alliance of "people of color"
    D. wanted to strengthen the Republican Party

22. Each of the following was an element of the Radical Republican program implemented during Reconstruction, EXCEPT   22.____

    A. the provision of 40 acres of land to each freedman
    B. military occupation of the South
    C. restrictions on presidential power
    D. punishment of Confederate leaders

23. In publishing *The Impending Crisis of the South* in 1857, Hilton Rowan Helper attempted to   23.____

    A. make the pragmatic argument that slavery actually harmed the Southern economy overall
    B. warn Northerners that Southern states were prepared to secede over the issue of slavery
    C. warn Southerners that the North was adopting an increasingly aggressive and militant posture, and invasion was imminent
    D. make an impassioned plea against the cruelty and immorality of slavery

24. Many historians argue that the Compromise of 1850, while it did not settle the issue of slavery in the United States,   24.____

    A. created a ten-year delay in which the South cashed in on its crops to build up a large surplus that effectively made the Civil War a longer and deadlier conflict than it might have been
    B. created a ten-year delay in which the North rapidly industrialized and grew more capable of defeating the South in military conflict
    C. was an effective means of dampening sectional divisions between North and South
    D. effectively discouraged any foreign powers from interfering in the issue of slavery in the United States

25. When George Henry White, the last Southern black of the post-Reconstruction period to serve in Congress, retired in _____, the U.S. Congress was completely white once again. 25.____

    A. 1888
    B. 1901
    C. 1917
    D. 1924

KEY (CORRECT ANSWERS)

1.	A	11.	D
2.	D	12.	B
3.	A	13.	B
4.	B	14.	C
5.	B	15.	A
6.	D	16.	A
7.	C	17.	B
8.	C	18.	A
9.	C	19.	B
10.	C	20.	D

21.	D
22.	A
23.	A
24.	B
25.	B

TEST 3

DIRECTIONS: Each question or incomplete statement is followed by several suggested answers or completions. Select the one that BEST answers the question or completes the statement. *PRINT THE LETTER OF THE CORRECT ANSWER IN THE SPACE AT THE RIGHT.*

1. In its Civil Rights Cases ruling of 1883, the Supreme Court ruled that
    I. the Thirteenth Amendment, while it outlawed the ownership of slaves, did not outlaw discriminatory behavior
    II. the "equal protection" provision of the Fourteenth Amendment applied to government but not private individuals and organizations
    III. "separate but equal" public facilities for black and white Americans were lawful
    IV. the Civil Rights Act of 1875, which required open access to all public accommodations, whether publicly or privately owned, was unconstitutional

    A. I and II
    B. I, II and IV
    C. III only
    D. I, II, III and IV

    1.____

2. The platform of the _____ Party during the 1860 election was that the South had a constitutional right to slavery, but Congress should not allow it to expand.

    A. Constitutional Union
    B. Northern Democratic
    C. Southern Democratic
    D. Republican

    2.____

3. When it was written, the Constitution of the Confederate State of America illustrated that a main philosophical difference between the North and South was the

    A. relationship of states to the national government
    B. impact of party politics
    C. universality of Supreme Court decisions
    D. power of the executive branch

    3.____

4. The term "slavocracy" was used

    A. to refer to the political power of slaveholding states in Congress
    B. by Northerners who resented the dominance of the issue of slavery over other significant political issues, which received scant attention
    C. by Southerners to refer to the sudden electoral significance of freed slaves
    D. to refer to the South's total dependence on the institution of slavery

    4.____

5. By 1870, free blacks comprised about _____ percent of the population of Washington,

    A. 10
    B. 30
    C. 50
    D. 70

    5.____

6. Of the terms offered by the Republicans to Southerners in the Compromise of 1877 in exchange for their recognition of Rutherford B. Hayes as president, the ones that ultimately took effect included
   I. the removal of all Federal troops from the former Confederate states
   II. the appointment of at least one Southern Democrat to Hayes' cabinet
   III. the construction of another transcontinental railroad using the Texas and Pacific in the South
   IV. legislation that would help industrialize the South

   A. I only
   B. I and II
   C. II and IV
   D. I, II, III and IV

7. *I answer that whenever it becomes necessary, in our growth and progress to acquire more territory, that I am in favor of it, without reference to the question of slavery, and when we have acquired it, I will leave the people free to do as they please, either to make it slave or free territory, as they prefer.*

   The words above were spoken in 1858 by

   A. Stephen A. Douglas
   B. Charles Sumner
   C. Abraham Lincoln
   D. James Buchanan

8. David Walker's *Appeal to the Colored Citizens of the World*, published in 1829,
   I. claimed that indifferent Christian ministers deserved some responsibility for slavery
   II. called for the immediate abolition of slavery
   III. urged slaves to kill their masters in order to win freedom
   IV. was vehemently opposed to recolonization

   A. I only
   B. II only
   C. II and III
   D. I, II, III and IV

9. The Underground Railroad became much more significant after the enactment of the

   A. Missouri Compromise of 1820
   B. Kansas-Nebraska Act of 1854
   C. Fugitive Slave Act of 1850
   D. Compromise of 1850

10. One of the primary motivations for Republicans to pass the Fifteenth Amendment was that they

    A. needed black voters in order to hang onto power
    B. wanted to prevent former Confederate officials from voting
    C. wanted to bring discriminatory practices such as poll taxes and literacy tests to a final end
    D. needed to deter the influence of the Ku Klux Klan over Southern politics

11. Abraham Lincoln denounced the _____ on the grounds that it "would amount to a perpetual covenant of war against every people, tribe, and state owning a foot of land between here and Tierra del Fuego."

    A. Kansas-Nebraska Act
    B. act of secession
    C. Crittenden Compromise
    D. Compromise of 1850

12. Anti-slavery sentiment was at the root of the formation of the _____ Party in 1840.

    A. Free Soil
    B. Liberty
    C. Republican
    D. Know-Nothing

13. Direct and indirect results of the American Civil War included
    I. improved standards of living for industrial workers
    II. broader scope of federal power
    III. expansion of women's roles and spheres of influence
    IV. increased government support for business and farming

    A. I and II
    B. II only
    C. II, III and IV
    D. I, II, III and IV

14. The Reconstruction-era Dunning School, a school of thought named after Columbia University professor William Archibald Dunning, contended that

    A. equal treatment for freedmen would naturally occur over time as human beings became more enlightened, but could not be compelled
    B. the only tool adequate for insuring and protecting the civil rights of freedmen was the federal government
    C. freedmen were incapable of self-government and had themselves made segregation necessary
    D. slavery had been a grievous sin that could only be atoned for through the enactment of special privileges for freedmen

15. The original organizer of the Compromise of 1850 was

    A. William Seward
    B. John Crittenden
    C. Lewis Cass
    D. Henry Clay

16. Lincoln's primary rival for the Republican nomination in 1860 was

    A. William Seward
    B. Salmon P. Chase
    C. John Bell
    D. Simor Cameron

17. The Personal Liberty Laws passed in northern states throughout the first half of the 19th century were designed to

    A. counteract the effects of the Fugitive Slave Law
    B. end the practice of imprisonment for debt
    C. encourage the abolition of slavery
    D. extend the rights of privacy to medical records

18. Each of the following battles was a part of (Grant's) Western Campaign, EXCEPT

    A. the Wilderness
    B. Fort Donelson
    C. Shiloh
    D. Perryville

19. The 54th Massachusetts Volunteer Infantry is famous for its Civil War service because it

    A. bore much of the responsibility for turning back Pickett's Charge
    B. was one of the only northern regiments to travel south and fight for the Confederacy
    C. one of the first official African-American units in the U.S. armed forces
    D. consisted entirely of unpaid soldiers

20. Once he was made General-in-Chief of the armed forces, Ulysses S. Grant's overall strategy for winning the war was to

    A. aggressively attack the seat of the Confederate government in Richmond and let the rest of the Confederacy fall as a result
    B. fight a total war that would permanently destroy the South's ability to fight
    C. start fighting the West and move eastward toward Virginia
    D. slowly starve the South by means of a naval blockade and avoid significant bloodshed

21. The Massachusetts Emigrant Aid Company, later the New England Emigrant Aid Company, was founded in 1854 in order to fight against the extension of slavery to _____ Territory.

    A. Kansas
    B. Nebraska
    C. New Mexico
    D. Utah

22. The Wilmot Proviso was endorsed by the _____ Party.
    I. Free Soil
    II. Democratic
    III. Republican
    IV. Know-Nothing

    A. I only
    B. I and III
    C. I, III and IV
    D. II and IV

23. In the Reconstruction-era South, 80 percent of Republican votes were supplied by

    A. freedmen
    B. scalawags
    C. carpetbaggers
    D. Redeemers

24. Booker T. Washington believed that the best way for African Americans to achieve economic and political rights was to

    A. use the existing U.S. court system
    B. emigrate from the United States and launch new societies elsewhere, preferably in Africa
    C. expand opportunities for vocational education
    D. launch an armed resistance against the oppressive government

25. "... the descendants of Africans who were imported into this country, and sold as slaves ... are not included, and were not intended to be included, under the word "citizens" in the Constitution, and can therefore claim none of the rights and privileges which that instrument provides for and secures to citizens of the United States ..."

    The text above is an excerpt from the

    A. Supreme Court's written opinion in its ailing in *Dred Scott v. Sandford*
    B. Supreme Court's written opinion in its ruling in *Plessy v. Ferguson*
    C. Missouri Compromise of 1820
    D. Kansas-Nebraska Act

KEY (CORRECT ANSWERS)

1.	B	11.	C
2.	A	12.	B
3.	A	13.	C
4.	A	14.	C
5.	B	15.	D
6.	B	16.	A
7.	A	17.	A
8.	D	18.	A
9.	C	19.	C
10.	A	20.	B

21. A
22. A
23. A
24. C
25. A

TEST 4

DIRECTIONS: Each question or incomplete statement is followed by several suggested answers or completions. Select the one that BEST answers the question or completes the statement. *PRINT THE LETTER OF THE CORRECT ANSWER IN THE SPACE AT THE RIGHT.*

1. Abraham Lincoln's fundamental argument against the secession of Southern states was that 1._____

    A. the U.S. government was a Union of people, and not states.
    B. slavery was cruel and could never be allowed in North America
    C. he had the constitutional responsibility to put down acts of sedition or rebellion
    D. the people of the Southern states had not been allowed to vote on secession

2. The _____ was a violent attempt by Southern whites to "persuade" white Republicans to join the Democratic Party, leaving the Republican Party as an African-American minority? 2._____

    A. Amnesty Act of 1872
    B. Compromise of 1877
    C. Poll Patrol of 1874
    D. Mississippi Plan of 1875

3. In their plan for Reconstruction, Abraham Lincoln and Andrew Johnson focused on 3._____

    A. Southern states' payment of reparations to the Union
    B. the participation of freed slaves in Southern political life
    C. Southern states' rapid re-entry into the Union
    D. punishment of the South for starting the Civil War

4. For both sides, the Civil War was financed largely by each of the following means, EXCEPT 4._____

    A. loans
    B. the sale of gold deposits
    C. taxes
    D. printing paper currency

5. The event that posed a direct challenge to Stephen A. Douglas's advocacy of popular sovereignty was the 5._____

    A. Kansas-Nebraska Act
    B. *Dred Scott* decision
    C. 1860 presidential election
    D. Freeport Doctrine

6. The Reconstruction Acts of 1867 provided for 6._____
    I. extensive loyalty oaths as a precondition of readmission to the Union
    II. ratification of the Fourteenth Amendment prior to readmission to the Union
    III. the registration of black voters
    IV. the creation of five military districts in the seceded states

A. I and II
B. I and IV
C. I, II and IV
D. I, II, III and IV

7. Confederate General Thomas J. Jackson earned the nickname "Stonewall" at the Battle of

   A. Fredericksburg
   B. Chancellorsville
   C. Mechanicsville
   D. First Bull Run (Manassas)

7.____

8. Ulysses S. Grant's 1868 election to the presidency was

   A. achieved through Grant's winning a substantial majority of white voters
   B. effected primarily because of the votes of former slaves
   C. interpreted as a sign that Southern states were ready to accommodate some of the aims of Reconstruction
   D. an overwhelming popular victory that nevertheless achieved a slim margin of victory in the Electoral College

8.____

9. In the early stages of the war, large prisoner-of-war camps were not used by either side because

   A. hardly any prisoners were taken
   B. the widespread practice of prisoner exchanges precluded the need for long-term arrangements
   C. prisoners of war were typically farmed out to rural areas to work as laborers
   D. it was widely known that such camps were a breeding ground for virulent diseases

9.____

10. Which of the following was NOT a battle of the Peninsula Campaign?

    A. Seven Pines
    B. First Bull Run
    C. Yorktown
    D. Hampton Roads

10.____

11. In proclaiming and implementing the Emancipation Proclamation, President Lincoln based his authority on the

    A. constitutional duties of the President of the United States
    B. Commerce Clause of the Constitution
    C. concept of natural law
    D. powers of the Commander-in-Chief of the Army and the Navy

11.____

12. Most accurately, the secessionist movement can be said to have been dominated by

    A. border-state moderates who could not support Lincoln's election
    B. extreme Southern nationalists who hoped to establish a separate plantation society
    C. hill-country white supremacists who feared the *entry* of blacks into civil society
    D. Southern moderates who wanted to keep the issue of slavery out of federal control

12.____

13. Which of the following was a result of the 1860 election?

    A. all four major party candidates won electoral votes
    B. John Bell carried two Northern states
    C. Northern votes were split fairly evenly between Lincoln and Douglas
    D. Lincoln won a majority of the popular vote

14. The Southern hunger for additional slave territory to counteract the effect of free territorial expansion was illustrated by William Walker's temporary takeover of the government in

    A. Santo Domingo
    B. Sonora
    C. Texas
    D. Nicaragua

15. After Reconstruction, the "New South" wanted the focus of its economy to be

    A. transportation
    B. crops other than cotton
    C. cotton
    D. industry

16. Which of the following events occurred FIRST?

    A. First Reconstruction Act
    B. Wade-David Bill
    C. Ulysses S. Grant's presidential election
    D. Fifteenth Amendment ratified

17. The U.S. slave population

    A. increased dramatically from 1800-1860
    B. declined somewhat after the Compromise of 1820
    C. grew at a relatively modest rate of about 2 or 3 percent a year for much of the first half of the 19th century
    D. remained relatively stable, as many Southern slaves were able to escape to the North or buy their freedom

18. One significant result of the Emancipation Proclamation was that

    A. several border states seceded from the Union
    B. many Republicans became disillusioned with Lincoln
    C. European nations decided not to support the Confederacy
    D. millions of slaves were freed throughout the South

19. It is generally true that the institution of slavery in the antebellum South

    A. was the source of constant tension between those who owned slaves and those who did not
    B. created a strong sense of community responsibility among whites
    C. created an egalitarian society among whites
    D. had the effect of devaluing free labor

20. The Civil War's "Gettysburg of the West" occurred at _____, where Henry Hopkins Sibley's Confederate forces were halted in their invasion of the West by Union forces under the command of Colonel Edward Canby.

    A. Bear River
    B. Glorieta Pass
    C. Tucson
    D. Valverde

21. Dred Scott was a slave who sued for his freedom on the grounds that

    A. he was captured after he had already been freed by his master
    B. slavery was unconstitutional
    C. he had offered a fair price to purchase his freedom from his master
    D. he had been a slave in a state where slavery was illegal

22. In order to decide the fate of slavery in the territories, the Kansas-Nebraska bill drafted by Stephen A. Douglas applied the same principle as the one used in the

    A. Wilmot Proviso
    B. Missouri Compromise
    C. Compromise of 1850
    D. Dred Scott decision

23. The reason that Abraham Lincoln famously suspended the writ of *habeas corpus* during the Civil War was that he wanted to

    A. have secessionists tried and convicted before military tribunals
    B. keep Kentucky from seceding from the Union
    C. forestall the Ku Klux Klan's influence in the South
    D. keep a group of Maryland secessionists in jail

24. During Reconstruction, Southern blacks most typically

    A. worked farms as renters and sharecroppers
    B. migrated northward
    C. owned and worked small farms
    D. worked as urban day laborers

25. The 1860 platform of the Republican Party included
    I. the abolition of slavery
    II. protective tariffs
    III. free homesteads
    IV. the construction of a transcontinental railroad

    A. I only
    B. I, II and IV
    C. II, III and IV
    D. I, II, III and IV

KEY (CORRECT ANSWERS)

1.	A	11.	D
2.	D	12.	D
3.	C	13.	A
4.	B	14.	D
5.	B	15.	D
6.	D	16.	B
7.	D	17.	A
8.	B	18.	C
9.	B	19.	D
10.	B	20.	B

21. D
22. C
23. D
24. A
25. C